Grassroots Football 1960-1980

by

Derek Hempshall

ISBN: 978-1-291-28961-9

Copyright © 2013 Derek Hempshall

All rights reserved, including the right to reproduce this book, or portions thereof in any form. No part of this text may be reproduced, transmitted, downloaded, decompiled, reverse engineered, or stored, in any form or introduced into any information storage and retrieval system, in any form or by any means, whether electronic or mechanical without the express written permission of the author.

PublishNation | London

www.publishnation.co.uk

I dedicate this book to my wife Eileen.
Her patience and fortitude is never ending.
With the publication of this book, at last,
I have managed to finish a job!

With thanks to: -

Reg Kimber
John Colledge
A D Colledge
John Clarke
Roger and Carol Hempshall
John Pinnegar
Bob Thompson
Vic Terry
John Adams
Rod Larcombe
Ray Staff
Edwin Greaves
Noel Rogers
Coventry Evening Telegraph
The History Centre Staff, Herbert Art Gallery and Museum

In memory of players and supporters who left the field of play before the final whistle was blown.

Paul (Chalkie) White – Apollo Rangers
Kevin Harridence – Apollo Rangers
Ken Robbins – Avondale FC
Jimmy Peterson – Barras Green WMC
John Phelan – Barras Green WMC
Dave McOwat – Barras Green WMC
Brian Clough – Barras Green WMC
Jim McQueen – Barras Green WMC
Terry Gaut – Parkstone WMC
Graham Fletcher – Parkstone WMC
Pete Fletcher – Parkstone WMC
Graham Meek – Wickman Limited

GRASSROOTS FOOTBALL 1960-1980

Part 1	Growing Pains	Page 1
	Early Football Experience	
	Mum and Dad	
	Girls	
	Work and Marriage	
Part 2	Meet the Teams	Page 23
	Moseley United	
	A C Godiva	
	Parkstone WMC	
	Avondale FC	
	Barras Green WMC	
	Apollo Rangers FC	
Part 3	Football Matters	Page 71
	Sunday Football	
	Referees	
	Injuries	
	Socialising	
	Laundry	
Part 4	Press Reports	Page 101
	Moseley United	
	A C Godiva	
	Parkstone WMC	
	Avondale FC	
	Barras Green WMC	
	Apollo Rangers FC	

Part 5	Results and Tables	Page 149
	Moseley United	
	A C Godiva	
	Parkstone WMC	
	Avondale FC	
	Barras Green WMC	
	Apollo Rangers FC	
Part 6	World Events 1960-1980	Page 208

Team Photographs

Introduction

Grassroots Football is the lowest level at which teenagers and adults can play soccer competitively. The Football League has a pyramid system, which is bound together by promotion and relegation. It is possible, in theory, for a lowly amateur club to rise to the pinnacle of the English game. This system does not include Sunday football.

Grassroots Football is not for professional or semi-professional players, it is for amateur players and is sometimes referred to as 'Junior' or 'Non-League' and comes under the jurisdiction of the Local Football Association. In the Coventry and District area, all football clubs are affiliated to the Birmingham FA.

I had recently retired and was looking for something to fill the time of day. The last twenty years was spent looking into a computer screen, so daytime television was out of the question! Before I left work, I had discussed my options with the two workmates, Dean Sturgess and Mike Tuckett, (I'm going to miss them!). Dean had said, "...you're good with letters, you should write a book". What a brilliant idea!

The inspiration to write this book came from a photograph published recently in the Coventry Evening Telegraph. The picture was of a local amateur football team, Grange United, who fifty years before, had played a game against a rival team, Longford Rangers. The match was played on a local parks pitch which was surrounded by possibly two thousand people, standing ten to fifteen deep. The atmosphere was electric! It was a 'David and Goliath' event, Grange United were the new kids on the block, and Longford Rangers were the Coventry Combination's top team for many years. The result of the game is not that important; in any case, there would be a return game the next week, and again the massed spectators weren't going to miss a tackle, or a goal.

The photograph reminded me of the cup final I had played in front of such a crowd, not on a parks pitch, but at the Butts Stadium in

Coventry. (Now rebuilt and the home of Coventry Rugby Club). Other memories followed, hence the book, a record of the 1960's and 70's, where football was an escape from the everyday routine of a teenage schoolboy passing along life's highway, with a future that offered a secure job and a marriage with 2.4 children! The cocoon of a secure and happy existence was not to be; it was all at the risk of world events, over which I had no control!

The British are sport mad, whether its football, rugby, cricket, tennis, cycling, horse racing, fishing, darts, snooker, skiing, yachting or athletics, or anything else you can name, we can't get enough. The medium of television allows anyone to view the sport that interests them, from the comfort of their armchairs. We can watch highly paid and highly skilled professional persons ply their trade, or support dedicated amateur individuals as they battle against the odds. Ideally, we should make the effort to go to venues to watch their efforts, and indeed we do, as stadiums around the country hold sixty to eighty thousand visitors. The organisation of these events has developed over hundreds of years, and is near infallible. From the comfort of our homes we can book tickets and arrange travel. All we need to do is turn up on time, and enjoy the event.

The summer Olympics were held in this country for the first time since 1948, and a whole cluster of new arenas were built in London and elsewhere. The spectacle encouraged more people to take up sport and exercise to lead a fitter and more active life, rather than watch athletes and footballers on television. The taking part is everything!

In 1966 we had the Football World Cup to look forward to. It was an event that resurrected the 'Dunkirk spirit' and united the nation; even more so, when England won the Jules Rimet Trophy, beating Germany.

It was significant the post-war 'baby boom' led to a surge in the number of amateur football teams all over the country. At the beginning of the sixties, there were a lot of teenagers with time on their hands, and football was better than hanging around on street corners. With the increase of the number of teams in the league, it was difficult for the leagues administrators to assess the strength of the new sides, and for a few years there would be weak teams in high divisions and strong teams in lower divisions. The other problem was - where would all the new teams play their football?

The emergence of the Coventry and District Sunday Football League put pressure onto the Parks and Leisure Department to provide new pitches. They had sufficient land to mark out new pitches, but didn't have adequate buildings for changing facilities. The cost of paying staff for two days at the weekend could be paid for by the football clubs. They coped somehow, but over the next twenty years, some of these facilities would disappear, not to be replaced; mainly because they were not fit for the purpose, or they had been vandalised beyond repair. The Stoke Heath changing rooms were one of the first buildings to be knocked down, and yet some of the pitches were still used for league matches; the players having to change in their cars along Mercer Avenue. Not satisfactory! In recent times, the City Council have just refurbished the changing rooms at the Memorial Park, as part of a big investment. I hope the showers work better than the previous ones!

I got a lot of enjoyment playing football during that period, and played nearly a thousand games. I still see some of the players I played with, and we always say that it would be nice to have a reunion, and chat about the good old days, because as we get older, we know more or less, what the future holds, and it is better to remember the past!

In writing this book, I wanted to talk about my experiences in amateur football and relate how it all fitted into the rest of my life. I hope that other footballers will read this, and be able to draw on their own memories. It isn't that easy to recall every goal you scored, or each match you played in, but if you take one season at a time, you will be able to recall the events that shaped your lives.

It is sad that former team-mates have passed away. I was aware of a few, but I was told of others, as I was researching the book, and I feel the loss.

Part 1 Growing Pains

Early Football Experiences

I was given a pair of football boots by my cousin, he was right footed – you didn't need to be Poiret to guess that – the toe cap on the right boot was worn away! The boots were one or two sizes too big, but I couldn't wait to try them out. I put on as many socks as I had and went into the garden. I had little option but to kick the ball with my left foot.

Football boots in the 1950's were not much different to the working man's hobnail boot, the back of the boot came up to cover and protect your ankle, and the studs were leather nailed into a thick leather sole. The nails had to be hammered flat on the inside of the boot, and were covered by a loose insole. The studs would wear easily if the owner walked on anything but turf, and eventually the nails would stand proud and could do some damage to an opponent's legs.

My first game with my "new" boots was for the 78th Wolf Cubs. We played at Partridge Croft home of the 7th group. The pitch was small compared to the one at school. The grass had not been cut for about two years (I'm sure that Doctor Livingstone was playing for the 7th). We chased the ball like a pack of wolves (pardon the pun) and eventually won 7-0.

Next game we played the 82nd at the back of St Laurence's Church, Bell Green and this time the pitch was in a field shaped like a bowl, and the opposition over-ran us and won 8-2. One of their players scored six.

The ability of teams in the Wolf Club league (yes there was a league!) depended on the age of their players. Wolf cubs could be seven to eleven years old and then they became Boy Scouts. It was disconcerting if your team had seven and eight year olds and were up against a side with ten year olds.

The 13th group at that time had a player who was ten and tall as a Poplar tree, he was skilful too. When we played them at Foleshill Park in Holbrooks (what a contradiction – it was renamed Holbrook Park only recently), the big chap scored ten goals in a 13-1 win. He was in a class of his own and could score more or less at will. My only memory of the game was his mother screaming at him on the touchline all through the game. God help him.

I went to Holbrook Primary School, and wasn't considered good enough to play in the school football team. I liked playing on the left wing, but the lad who played in that position, John Burkitt, later went on to play left back for Coventry City. We had two other good footballers, Peter Woodcock and Alan Setchell. I would meet up with Alan five years later, playing for Moseley United.

Just before I left to go to secondary school, the sports teacher arranged a match against local rivals Edgewick to ensure that the rest of the boys got a game. Our school pitch was surrounded by the Dunlop, Motor Panels and Ernest Batley factories, and the workers would line up at the fence to watch the games when the left work. I played in my preferred position on the left wing and really enjoyed the game, I had a chance to score in a breakaway but the centre forward got his foot to the ball first and pushed it past their goalie into the net. The game ended in a 1-1 draw.

My secondary school was Foxford Comprehensive, in Longford. We could only play Rugby in the first year. I didn't go much for the tackling or the rucking and scrimmages, but I could kick and catch the odd shaped ball. We had one match arranged against the Barker Butts School at Coundon Road on a pitch next to the Coventry Rugby Club's ground. We didn't know that Barkers had a strong rugby tradition and we were comprehensively beaten. I played Hooker and got crushed in amongst the big boys, and I didn't get much chance to hoof the ball. One of the sports teachers thought I would make a good full back, and he taught me how to kick a rugby ball and catch it properly, unfortunately I never got chance to put it into practice on the rugby pitch, but it did help on the football pitch when taking goal kicks and free kicks for distance.

I didn't get much chance to play football at school, only at play time. The pitches had only recently been laid and didn't drain very well. The local brook, which ran through the school, would also overflow.

With no football we had to have cross country running. The route from the school took us past the Wyken Slough, a body of water that was fed by the small tributary of the river Sowe. After heavy rain, the track which crossed the river at a ford would be under two foot of flood water, and we had to wade through it. Then there was a steep uphill climb to the "Clog banks", an area which was basically spoil from mine workings, clay and coal dust. The run went on back around the Slough and to the school, about three miles. Good exercise but not pleasant.

Some of the football mad lads in the fourth and fifth years were playing on Saturdays in the Coventry Youth League. It didn't appeal to me at the time as I was happy to have a kick-about with friends, or watch a game on Longford Park.

I spent many hours on the park, at that time it had two football pitches, tennis courts, bowling green and a pitch and putt course. The river Sowe ran through it, and when it was in spate, it was touch and go as to whether you could get across the bridge to get to school.

Most lads have a best mate, you could have more than one best mate - it was allowed. Girls didn't have best mates because they're fickle. In my case I had one best mate for 'at school', and for 'after school and weekends'. At school my best mate was Dave Collins who lived in Rowleys Green, and for after school and weekends, my best mate was John Colledge, he lived just up the road from me in Lythalls Lane, but went to Whitley Abbey School. Best mates talked the same language, knew what the other was thinking and wanted what you wanted. As far as I know my best mates never met, there was no need for them to meet.

Dave and I were in the same house (Neptune) and Set (One) at school and sat together in lessons, we had the same interests and we went to the same church and youth club. ("That's not allowed", you might say, "its' after school and weekends". Yes you're right of course, but we make the rules, and they can be changed!). I lost touch with Dave when we left school, and saw him fleetingly once when he applied for a job at Wickman.

John and I would kick a football around Longford Park for hours on end. We would take turns as goalie or striker, assuming the name of the current star professional player. Neither of us was any good in goal, but it didn't matter. As the striker you were the star and celebrated each goal scored. We practised free kicks swerving the ball in either direction, using the instep or outside of the foot, and took penalties until we dropped. Other times, we just dribbled around, trying to keep the ball, or winning it back.

I had other hobbies that John wasn't into, such as train spotting and fishing. Both hobbies could be enjoyed singularly, or with friends. I used to go to Bulkington to watch the steam engines power round the curve through the old station, on their way to London and all points north. The Royal Scot, The Red Rose, The Coronation Scot, The Caledonian, The Mancunian, and The Mid-day Scot. Marvellous!

I would also spend hours alongside the Coventry Canal dangling my maggots. I used to meet up with the Parkstone lads, namely Dave (Seff) Sephton, Pete (Percy) Preston, Roger Wells (Wellsy), Bobby Gubbins, Tony (Wiff) Smith and Roland Clegg (Cleggy). We used to fish under the Longford Road bridge, by the old Foleshill Gas Works. We 'rescued' a girl from the canal one day; she was cycling along the towpath, lost control of her bike and went in the water. It was about four to five feet deep, and she was close enough to the side for us to pull her out. We also managed to get her bike out of 'the cut', and off she went, dripping wet and a bit embarrassed, without a thank you! It ruined the fishing, but we couldn't stop laughing for days.

The Parkstone lads would play football on the Longford Park, Bobby wasn't good at football and usually went in goal, Pete was a big lad nearly as wide as tall, and you didn't want to get in his way, Seff, Wellsy, Cleggy and Wiff were reasonably good and showed promise. Sometimes other lads would join in and start a game; on some occasions it would go on until it was dark, and we had fifteen or more on each side, all ages and sizes. It was difficult to know whose side you were on!

In the summer it was too hot for football, so we used to played cricket, Tip-it and Run. One day, Wellsy batted all afternoon, and scored three hundred and sixty five, or more. Nobody could get him out! We must have covered every blade of grass and searched the brook for the ball.

That area of the park was where the smaller football pitch was. It was on a slope which dipped sharply down in one corner toward the brook. It was a tight pitch restricted by the brook and the pathway through the park. The larger pitch was flat apart from one touchline which was still a bit ridge and furrow from the original farmland.

That pitch was used on Saturdays by Longford Rangers FC. They ran two successful teams in the Coventry Combination League. They were based at the Old Crown Inn on Windmill Road, which was run by Jack Snape, a former Coventry City player; his two sons, Dave and Mick were at Foxford School at that time, and both had good skills.

Most Saturdays, we would watch the Rangers play, and they had a good centre forward, Pat Hurren. He was not that tall and of slight build, but he knew how to look after himself, and put the ball in the net.

At half-time we would take our football and 'shoot-in' the goal. The football club had put up nets and when the ball hit the back of the nets, it was like the real thing.

The matches between Longford Rangers and Grange United (described in the Introduction) took place in my final year at school, and soon I would be playing 'real' football every Saturday.

Mum and Dad

Mum and Dad lived through two World wars, although they were quite young when the 1914-18 war commenced. They first met when they were working at Courtaulds making munitions during the second war. They both worked long shifts on Capstan Lathes, and Dad was also on Fire Watch with the Home Guard. They were married in 1941 and my brother, Roger was born in 1944. I was a "Victory baby" along with thousands of others in the post-war baby boom. Mum was forty when she gave birth to me.

We lived in Beresford Avenue and our garden backed onto a railway line, known as the Coventry Loop, it was an avoiding line for freight to go between Nuneaton and Rugby without passing through Coventry Station. Both Roger and I became avid trainspotters, and still are. (The A444 Phoenix Way replaced the railway line).

Post war Britain was a busy place with lots of rebuilding to be done, but there was also a lot of unemployment as troops came home and were "demobbed", and there was no longer the need for all the factory workers, or the demand for warplanes and ammunition.

Dad was a Slater by trade when I was born, and Mum stayed at home to look after us kids. Dad later went to work at Morris Engines in Courthouse Green, and we moved house to Booths Fields, a footpath that runs between Foleshill Road and Lythalls Lane. Dad was working a forty-eight hour shift, and smoked at least forty cigarettes a day. He used to cough a lot, but blamed it on the Cast Iron dust from the machining of Cylinder Blocks at work.

Work done, after dinner and forty winks, he would go for a drink at The Heath public house or the Edgewick Trades Hall Club. In those times, most men worked and went to the pub, and the wife stayed at home to look after the kids.

Works holidays amounted to two weeks in July and Christmas day. As a result, most of the children in the fifties were born in April or September.

We only had two holidays in sixteen years, the first was a coach trip to Rhyl; it rained all day! The second was a glorious week in Gorleston-on-Sea near Great Yarmouth, I was seven at the time, Mum bought me a toy yacht and a ball of string; I spent hours each day pulling this yacht around a boating lake on the promenade. Great fun; kids today don't know what they're missing!

The Edgewick Club organised children's outings to Wicksteed Park. I went on two or three of them, but spent most of the day watching main line expresses pass by on a nearby railway line.

At Christmas, Morris Motors would also have parties for their employees' children, after some food there would be Abbott and Costello films.

Mum and Dad weren't strict, but they taught us right from wrong, and to respect other people and their property. Mum only shouted at us if we had broken a piece of her china, or a vase. She never smacked us because she had Rheumatoid Arthritis, and it would have hurt her more than us, so she used to threaten us with the rolling pin.

I loved my Mum, even though I played her up something terrible in my schooldays. I don't know how she managed to do the housekeeping, washing and ironing, shopping and cooking, with her swollen joints. She had to have operations on both her feet on the same day, which put her in bed for weeks and it took her a long time to learn how to walk again.

I did try to help as I grew up, I could dolly the washing in the big tub, and use the mangle to squeeze the water out of the clothes and sheets: no washing machines in those days!

All our clothes had to last, and were hand-me-downs, she would darn socks, and stitch collars, and knit woollen jumpers. When she had some spare time she would do some embroidery. At that time, paper patterns were available. The pattern was placed on the material and ironed, the ink of the pattern was then transferred to the material. Mum had a large tablecloth to sew with flowers and leaves and berries, quite beautiful. She let me stitch some of the easier shapes.

When Roger and I started playing football, the dirty kit would have to be put into soak immediately, to have any chance of removing the grass stains. The next day they would be washed and ironed, thank you Mum.

We had some pocket money when we went to secondary school, usually a theepenny bit (just over 1p in todays money), and when we were thirteen we could have a paper round, delivering morning and evening, before and after school.

Mum wasn't impressed when I told her my first school joke, "What's the definition of a Goldfish bowl – a pregnant jam jar". She said she didn't like what they were teaching me at school.

Both Roger and I went to Holbrooks and Foxford schools. We got a good education, which enabled us to get employment for all our working lives. I was quite proud of my achievements at school, but disappointed with my O level results, and I had a career to look forward to.

Dad was up early in the morning and got home from work about five thirty. After his dinner, Roger would finish off anything left on the plate, and Dad would then have a cup of tea and a fag, and would fall asleep. At seven on the dot he would wake up, wash, shave and change his clothes, and then go to the Heath pub on Foleshill Road. At weekends he would study form (a horse racing term) and fill out his halfpenny each way betting slips, and then away to the pub via the bookies.

I only asked my dad for three things, the first was to get me a ticket for the Coventry City versus Manchester United sixth round FA Cup match at Highfield Road. What a game, with stars like Bobby Charlton, Denis Law, Paddy Crerand, and Maurice Setters on show. For me the man of the match was Johnny Giles who went on to be the inspiration for Don Revie's Leeds United team. Coventry lost 3-1 in front of forty four thousand fans.

My next request, was for dad to attend an interview with me at Wickman, where I was offered an apprenticeship, and dad had to sign the Indenture forms. He had to take time off work, which was difficult in those times.

It was Grand National day 1967, and also Moseley United's day trip to London. I asked dad to put a £1 each way bet on a horse called Foinavon, which was an outsider at 100/1 odds. My chargehand, at work had read in the Daily Mirror, that the horse had a good chance if given a clear run. Dad said it had no chance, but if I left the pound he would place the bet. In my haste to catch the train, I forgot about leaving my stake. It wasn't until the late afternoon, that I saw the headlines in the Evening News, of how a lot of horses had fallen at the National and Foinavon had plodded along missing all the chaos and strolled home the winner. Then it dawned on me that I hadn't left dad my money. My luck was in again when he gave me my £67 winnings. Thank you dad!

My brother, Roger is two and a half years older than me. He played regular football on Saturdays for St Lawrences in the Youth League. There was only one division of eight teams, and the age of the players ranged from eleven to sixteen. (Nowadays the youth leagues are separated into age divisions).

When he left school, he went work at Cash's and played for their football team Kingfield, in the Works League, which had three divisions. The teams played on some of the best pitches in Coventry, owned by the major engineering companies in the city, such as Alvis, Brico, Cash's, Courtaulds, Dowty Sports, Dunlop, GEC, Herberts, Humber, Massey Ferguson, Morris, Municipal Sports, Renold Chain, Sphinx, Standard Triumph, and Wickman.

Roger played mostly at wing half and centre half throughout his career. He was a better player than me. A good reader of the game, solid and rarely missed a tackle, he was an excellent passer of the ball, and good in the air. These skills made him a respected player in the Works League.

When I started work at Wickman, I asked him if I would be good enough to play in the Works League, he said that I would get battered. He did point out that there were ex and semi-professionals playing for teams in that league, and they knew the tricks of the trade!

I was asked by some of the Wickman footballers to go training, but I was a bit reluctant. I was introduced to Reg Kimber who worked in the Sales office and was secretary of Moseley United FC (MUFC). After a chat, I agreed to turn up the next Saturday, because they might be short of players for their reserve match. Moseley United ran two teams in the Coventry and District League and played home games on local parks pitches. Away games could be at Fillongley, Kenilworth, Leamington, Stoneleigh, Baginton or Berkswell.

My best mate, John and I, played for Moseley United FC, Godiva FC and Apollo Rangers (later to become Colliers FC). John's first game for Moseley United Reserves, was two weeks after my debut. We were playing at Bubbenhall (we were not renting the pitch at this time), and opponents were Baginton British Legion. John's first action was a classic sliding tackle at speed, taking the ball cleanly. The opponent jumped in the air to avoid John. With this type of tackle it was always likely that your inertia would result in a collision with the opponent. Whether you were the tackler or the tackled, you just got on with the game. There was none of this rolling about on the ground with arms threshing in the air. It was acceptable for the opponent to try to return the favour.

There I was, starting out on my working career, and playing amateur football alongside my best mate. What more would anyone want?

Girls

When I was growing up, my first girlfriend was Carol who lived in Arbury Avenue. We were about twelve and used to play at Peggy's Park, a small area off Bedlam Lane. It had swings and slides, big and small, and a see-saw. The grassed areas were just about good enough for football and cricket, but there were some good trees to climb nearby, and the railway line ran past the bottom end of the park. Carol had a brother, who was into motorbikes, I was wary of him when he had his biking leathers on! The park was quite popular with all ages and generally everybody knew each other.

Carol and I got talking one day, and then seemed to be together every day for some time. She was quite tall and slender and pretty, and we liked holding hands and kissing. It didn't last, I don't quite know what caused the break up, but I blamed my brother, Roger. I can still remember Carol's kisses; her lips were soft and tasted nice, probably of tooth paste!

Talking of oral hygiene, or lack of it, my teeth were decaying fast, mainly due to lack of toothpaste after the war and sweet orange juice that was supplied by the local health service. My first visit to the dentist was frightening, and I had to have six of my front teeth extracted, and six others filled. The gap at the front of my mouth was filled with partial dentures top and bottom. This didn't do my confidence much good, and I steered clear of girls for a while. I met a girl who had part dentures herself and I thought that having a shared problem might be good for the both of us, but it was doomed to fail.

In my fourth year at school, when I was trying so hard to get my homework done and revise for my Pre-Tech exams, there was a girl that turned my head, we met by the chip shop in Lythalls Lane. A lad who lived at the top of our street, Dave, was with a girl, Sheila who I knew from Foxford School. Her friend Gillian, was playing 'gooseberry'. I spoke to them and Gillian was very friendly and we talked for several hours. I walked Gillian back home to Eld Road, and made arrangements to see her again. It was good for a while; then I was getting in very late and my homework was being neglected.

I did see Gillian a few years later, she got of a bus at Cross Road just as I walked past. Unfortunately, I had just had the rest of my teeth taken out and was not feeling too good and spitting blood. We should have met at a different time in our lives!

Some months later I fell in love with Susan who lived in Windmill Road. It was bad timing as I was due to take my "O" levels. She had lovely eyes (I found out years later, that the local lads called her Moon Eyes). We got on well at school and had a lot in common. Her mum was a barmaid at the New Inn Pub and her dad liked a drink, so in the evenings Susan had to stay in and look after he younger brother and two sisters. Not good news if you want to snog your girlfriend in the front room. I found it difficult to cope with the younger children, I didn't have younger brothers and sisters at home. Sometimes I would stay in with her, or if I was playing football in the park, she would come down to watch for a while. When we left school, Susan got a job at Dunlop and started immediately, whereas my job at Wickman didn't start for another two months. After I started work, I used to meet her out of work on a Friday afternoon, and walk her home. We continued meeting at her house and that's where I was on November 22nd 1963, when J F Kennedy was assassinated.

I think that Susan had her eyes opened further when she started work, and wanted something better than an apprentice as a boyfriend. Que Sera Sera. I was a bit upset at the time, but best mate John came and sorted me out. He took me down the park and I kicked hell out the ball!

A couple of years later I was introduced to Eileen on a Blind Date (Cilla was not there, she was off doing her singing stint). John Colledge and his girlfriend at the time, Lyn, had arranged the meeting at Lyn's house. Lyn and Eileen worked at the GEC works at Helen Street winding armatures for telephone systems. We arranged to go to the pictures to see Ken Russell's "Women in Love", a bit of a racy film, with nudity, sex and violence. Our romance blossomed as they say. John and Lyn drifted apart.

I was usually working overtime and got home late during the week, so we used to meet up at weekends. We would go for a drink at a local pub. Eileen lived in Little Field, Stoke Heath so we sometimes went to The Rose and Woodbine in North Street, or the Old Hall in Lythalls Lane, where there was a juke box. We would be joined by other couples and play the B sides of the latest hits. The other pub we visited regularly was The Heath on Foleshill Road. We went in the Rainbow room at the back of the pub. At weekends, they would have live music, usually a four piece band, which was different.

Girls, what do they give to football? Well quite a lot actually! Back in the 1960's girls who kicked a ball around were "tomboys" and "they would grow out of it" Nobody could foresee that there would be a FA Women's Super League in football.

Work and Marriage

When I started my career, I had to cycle about eight miles from Foleshill to the Wickman Machine Tool Company in Banner Lane, Tile Hill. It took about thirty minutes with the wind behind me. Alternatively, I could catch the bus into the city centre and catch one of the Wickman buses, which collected passengers along Tile Hill Lane and Broad Lane. These buses were additional to the existing services but went the extra mile up Banner Lane, and the Wickman drive with its manicured lawns and colourful flower beds, to deposit their passengers outside the office blocks.

My first pay packet was £3 6s 8d less tax. My first year was in the drawing office, and there were three apprentices to about fifty draughtsmen, and estimators. In between learning our trade, we had to distribute tea and coffee from the catering trolley to the men, and fetch confectionery etc from the canteen shop. I was transferred to the apprentice training school at Fletchamstead Highway, and learned how to operate a variety of machines and produce quality precision parts. Six months later, I was moved back to Banner Lane main workshop, where I worked on different sections such Cam Milling, Grinding, Drilling, and Inspection. I returned to the drawing office, for my last year, working on the Single Spindle section. I already knew most of the draughtsman on that section so I settled in easily.

I bought a motorbike from a chap at work, a Honda 50 Sports. Honda was flooding the UK with cheap small motorbikes that the public couldn't get or afford from Triumph, BSA and Royal Enfield etc., who only wanted to sell you a 500 Twin. I passed my test on the Honda, and I rode miles on that bike. It was off the road at times, mainly due to the pistons blowing. I traded up to a BSA Bantam Sports, this had a 175cc two- stroke engine, and you had to mix the petrol with two stroke oil. I could never get the mixture right, one day it would fly to work, the next day it would splutter and exhaust clouds of smoke. I eventually seized the engine, had to have it rebored with a new piston, then I got rid.

I had other motorcycles, both in need of repair. The first was a Royal Enfield Prince, a 150cc two-stroke that had a broken crankcase where the kick start pedal was. It took me over six months to obtain a replacement part. Dad was moaning at me because he couldn't get into "his" shed. The engine was rebuilt and the bike sold. The second bike was a Triumph Tiger Cub 200cc four-stroke. This came with a bent gear selector plate, which was easily repaired, but the bike also had a seized rear suspension arm. I couldn't fix it, so I passed it on to a workmate, who eventually freed it, by using a blow torch and a big hammer. No more motorcycles after that!

I used to turn up at Eileen's house either on foot, riding my bicycle, or pushing my motorbike. My mate John had the right idea - he bought a car! That was to be my next purchase; I bought a Standard 8 from a Wally Cure in the office at work for £25. The engine had been reconditioned and purred, but the bodywork was in need of repair, the wings especially. (The MOT test didn't exist then).

I needed to pass my test first, but I was working overtime and didn't get home till late, and my qualified driver John had moved on from girlfriend Lyn, and was spending all his time getting to know new girlfriend, Pat. To get some driving hours I used the car to get to Floyds Fields where Moseley United were playing Tile Hill. John was in front, and Eileen and Pat, were in the back. I parked the car near to the pitch so that the girls could watch us play football. Pat also worked at the GEC, so she and Eileen had plenty to talk about. After the match we returned to the car to find the rear tyre flat. Neither of the girls realised that the tyre had gone down, and they were so busy chatting that they never watched the game. We had a spare and changed the wheel, and drove home in silence.

Later I changed the two badly worn tyres for remoulds, and I was finding out the true cost of running a car, on apprentice pay. I couldn't afford to pay for the wings, so I sold the car to one of the regulars in the pub for a fiver profit. His lad restored the car to showroom condition and drove around in it for some years.

With my further education and my apprenticeship finished and my future secure with full employment in the Wickman Drawing Office on a salary of £21 per week, I saved hard to put a deposit on a house being built in Courthouse Green. The house was completed in May and we got married at the Registry Office in August 1970. We had the reception in the Rose and Woodbine in North Street, and that's when I was introduced to Eileen's six aunties and her relatives from Hartlepool. Eileen's mum hadn't been well for some time, but she gave us a short lesson on how to play the drums. We all had a good day, and as the party moved elsewhere, we slipped away quietly to our new house.

Wedded bliss was shattered five months later when Eileen's mum died. It was so sudden, and not related to her previous illness. She had woken her husband that morning complaining of feeling unwell, and before he could do anything - she had gone. Eileen took a long time to come to terms with her loss, and I didn't know how to ease her grief. After we had married, Eileen had always called into see her mum on the way home from work, now she had to support her Dad and brother, both were working men, and not used to housekeeping. To make sure that they had at least one square meal, they would come to ours for Sunday dinner. She also helped with their housework as well. The stress and grief was too much for her, and at work her job had changed. The new work was not to her liking, and she had to take time off work. My job was going well, there was a big Russian order for machines and tooling, and Britain was going Metric, and that meant there was plenty of overtime available and with the extra money, we made the decision for Eileen to finish work.

I was working sometimes three hours extra a day, the company provided "overtime teas" for the staff, which include tea and coffee, sandwiches and my favourite poached egg on toast. Working overtime, presented other problems, inasmuch that we were reliant on normal bus timetables, and not the Wickman special service. If I missed the bus into the city centre, I would have to wait at least twenty minutes for the next one. Then I had to catch another bus to Stoke Heath. By the time I got home it was time to get up!

When we got married, we didn't have a honeymoon, but the next year, we went to Llandudno for two weeks, a bit too Victorian for two young people, but we got on well with two other couples in the Hotel, and we went on local coach trips to Snowdon, Caenarvon and Betws-y-Coed. The evening entertainment was quite poor, both in the town and the hotel, but the holiday did both of us the world of good.

We decided to start a family and Wendy Dawn was born in September 1972. I wasn't at the birth, but I was playing football for

Barras Green WMC, and scored from a penalty at the time Wendy was delivered! That didn't impress Eileen.

I was smoking about twenty cigarettes a day, and decided to pack it in. I attended a 'No Smoking' course at the Local Ambulance Centre. This ran for five days and was after work. It was agreed at the first meeting for all attendees to hand over all their fags and never smoke again. The speakers talked about lung cancer, and showed films of operations to remove parts of lungs. They also talked about diet and ways of overcoming the need for a cigarette. They suggested that we should go on a fruit diet for a week, and take a drink of water if we wanted a fag. No tea or coffee. The other problem was "association"; when we go for a beer, we have a fag, after dinner we have a fag, we go upstairs on the bus so we can smoke. (It was allowed then). It was up to us to fight these associations and basically changed your lifestyle. I had a cold (again) and I managed to quit - but I wanted to. The fruit diet worked well, but there were a few strong smells in the office at work. Drinking water was also a good idea, but I couldn't get the pictures of the operation out of my head. About a year later a chap came to work on the drawing board next to me, and he had an operation to remove half of one lung, and showed me the scar, which ran from the nape of his neck down his back, and round the front under his ribs. Not nice! He had TB (tubercolosis).

Around that time, the Oil Crisis became a big issue, (so what's new). Prior to this event, prices of petrol and household shopping had risen, but with minimal effect, probably due the old currency when we had smaller coinage, such as the halfpenny and farthing. With decimalisation we had the 1/2p, which was worth 1.2 old pennies, so price increases were far more noticeable.

The Oil Shieks said that their oil reserves were dwindling and they would be cutting supplies and increasing charges. Britain had its own oil fields under the North Sea, but these were still being assessed. (It turned out to be the wrong type of crude, but we did get natural gas as a bonus). This was quickly followed by the three day week. The oil fired power stations quickly ran out of fuel, and power cuts and blackouts followed. Nobody was exempt, and we were give information of when we would have, and not have, electricity. The factories were also affected, and it became a major operation to juggle manpower. At Wickman, not only did the workers have to change their shift times, but office personnel were asked to work in natural light and without heat. No problem – we're British!

Inflation was rising and the unions were angry and wanted wages to follow suit. The Government of the day introduced a wage increase structure tied to the rate of inflation. So inflation rose and earning rose in line, which increased inflation etc. etc. Eventually the situation resolved itself, sort of, but the good life had gone, and the word Recession had replaced Fuel Crisis. Wickman were fortunate, they had another Russian order to process, but the death knell was starting to toll at many of Coventry's Engineering plants.

My fellow draughtsmen felt it was time for me to get some wheels! I had passed my motor bike test, which enabled me to drive a three wheeled vehicle. A neighbour, of Dick Richards, had a Reliant Regal 3/25. (This was the saloon version of Delboy Trotter's van, in the TV series "Only Fools and Horses"). The car had been off the road for some time. It needed a change of oil and filter, a set of plugs and points, and a new battery. I bought the necessary items and we fired it up. Bingo!

The MOT test had been recently introduced although it was not as severe in the beginning. I arranged for some car insurance, and Dick agreed to take the car to Astons in Far Gosford Street, the local Reliant dealer, for the MOT test. I collected it on my way home from work and paid the bill. Much to my surprise, it had passed, and I had to drive it home, in the rush hour. I hadn't driven since my Standard 8 days, and was bricking it.

My workmates had told me to make sure that the engine was warmed up, giving less chance of stalling. Warm up complete, no stalling, I joined the procession of traffic up Far Gosford Street and onto Walsgrave Road; both up hill. I didn't have experience at hill starts, so I kept the car in gear and slipped the clutch, whilst keeping the revs up. Suddenly, there were lights flashing on the dashboard, and orange lights flashing around the car. I pulled up and found all the indicator lights were flashing. There was very little that I could do, but the car was drivable, so I got home as fast as I could! I took the car to a local car electrics centre and they cleaned all the earth connections. Hey presto, I was mobile!

I trundled back and forward to work, and Eileen liked to be driven around the countryside, she would sit in the back with Wendy. One day we were driving toward Shilton and climbing a hill, there was an almighty bang and the car lost drive, and the engine stopped abruptly. I tried to start the engine and there was a loud metallic noise of two large pieces of iron banging against each other. We were not in the AA or the RAC, so decided to turn the car around and push it home. Reliants are basically a steel chassis and drive train, and a fibreglass body; so it didn't take much to get it rolling. We were at the top of this hill and I sat at the wheel, and Eileen gave a good push and away we went, leaving Eileen to catch up. Wendy was kneeling on the back seat, shouting "Mummy, Mummy". (We can still picture that, and have a laugh about it).

We were lucky that the road home was downhill to the last half a mile or so, then we needed some more bodies to get it up the last two hills to home. I pushed the car into the garage exhausted, and went up the pub. The chaps at work were very concerned, because they had put a lot of effort into getting the car on the road. They were of the opinion that a piston rod had snapped, or worse still, the crankshaft had broken! I was about to get a crash course in Car Servicing.

I bought some Axle stands and borrowed a pulley block and tackle. I had a 6x2 wooden beam in the garage and secured the pulley block to it. I stripped everything off the engine that I could and supported it with the lifting tackle. In a series of lifts I managed to raise the front of the body of the car, and enable me to lower the engine onto a skid and roll it away from the car. In hindsight, not very clever, but it worked. I separated the gearbox from the engine, and then the sump from the block, and the damage was revealed, the crankshaft had indeed snapped near to one of the bearing journals. I managed to get an old crankshaft for free, and had it reground. With the engine back together, it was not an easy job to get it back in the car, but with a lot of swearing and straining, it was done, and it was back on the road.

Some other lads at work had Reliant three wheelers as well, but the new Robin model, which had a smoother shape and a larger engine capacity. I was so impressed that I bought one. (This was to be my only new car). A friend of a friend bought the old reliant from me, and about a year later, yes, you've guessed it, the crankshaft broke!

The new Reliant cost £1100 and had alloy wheels! We went on several holidays in it. The first was to Barmouth; a chap in the office at work had a caravan on a site there and we hired it for a week, unfortunately Wendy was poorly sick by Wednesday, and Eileen insisted we went home. Wendy had measles so it was for the best that we returned.

We also went to Bournemouth, we stayed at the home of a former apprentice Brian Forward, who had moved from Coventry and changed careers also. My Mum and Dad went down on the train, and stayed there also, and all five of us crammed into the Reliant to visit the surrounding areas.

I managed to pass my full driving test, after taking some lessons with Sean at Easi-Drive. He realised that I was a competent driver, and he just taught me what I need to do to get a pass. On test day, I was first away, and it was over so quick, the examiner was impressed and gave me the pink slip. Sean was amazed to hear that I didn't have to reverse around a corner, something that he made me do time and again.

I traded the Reliant in for a "real" car, an Austin Allegro. Later, I had other Austin-Morris cars, the Marina and the Princess, all in a short space of time. They were all good cars, plenty of room, but they rusted badly. The Princess was a good motor for holidaying, it was comfortable and had lots of boot space. Mum liked the front seat, and said she felt like the queen!

I had my first crash in the Princess, a car pulled out in front of me from a line of parked cars, and forced me into the rear crash bar of lorry parked across the road. The car driver apologised and we exchanged insurance details. The lorry wasn't damaged, but my lovely Princess had two crumpled wings and a broken headlight.

At work, by 1977 I was looking to change jobs, I had tried to move to a different department, but the move was blocked by my Manager. I was told of a vacancy at a small contract design office, Enco Designs Limited, in the Stoke area. I had been to interviews before at contract offices, and had been told that I didn't have the experience to do that type of work. I attended the interview and made a good impression and got on well with the manager, Bob Haywood. I started work there later that month, and enjoyed the work and settled in quickly.

During the fourteen years at Wickman, I was fortunate to work with some of the nicest people you could wish for. My fellow draughtsmen on the Single Spindle section, gave me most pleasure, we could talk about anything, mainly other peoples misfortune, and at times it was hilarious, but at the same time being industrious and inventing some of the most innovative pieces of equipment for various type of machines. I was able to carry all their knowledge with me and use it in future employment. Thank you, Mick Wilkins, Terry Lloyd, Wally Cure, Jim O'Brien, Tony Saunders, Phil Barlow, Dick Richards, Keith Sedgebear, and Dave Entwistle.

Back at Wickman, my departure had repercussions in that the work I had been doing for the EDM department had been stopped, and no one could be made available to restart it. The situation was resolved at board level, and resulted in Wickman EDM asking me to work for them. I was a bit flattered and also in a bit of a quandary.

I decided to take up their offer, and left Enco Designs after six months; but I had agreed to work part time for them. (I would work for Enco part and fulltime for another seventeen years). Wickman EDM was based in Wyken, nearer home for me. I was the only designer and worked for Jim Homer, who had progressed through the Wickman management trainee system. Six months later Jim died suddenly, he was only a couple of years older than me. In a small company, the loss was devastating. I stayed for another two years and left before the site closed.

Clare Louise was born in May 1979. Eileen had woken that day, and her waters broke. I contacted the Maternity Unit and I was told to bring her straight in. The petrol gauge wasn't working in the Princess so I stopped at Barras Filling Station to make sure that I could get to the hospital. There was some strange looks on the faces of the other customers, Eileen was laid out on the back seat, screaming. We got to the Hospital, and parking was as bad then as it is now, and we eventually got to Maternity. A passing Midwife helped Eileen to the Reception desk, and I settled down for a long wait. Seconds later I was being whisked along corridors, trying to put on one of the stupid gowns that tie up at the back. In the Labour ward I was told to "Sit there" and baby Clare popped out almost immediately. Just like shelling peas!

I had stopped playing football by this time, the stress at work, wasn't helping much and all my joints were seizing up. I had been referred to the Hospital and the symptoms confirmed as Rheumatoid Arthritis.

I went to visit Eileen and Clare, that evening. Wendy had played up, she didn't understand that it was Fathers only visiting in the evening, and she wanted to see her mum and new sister. She didn't want to stay with friends of ours while I was out, so I had to take her to my brother Roger's house in Bedwoth. The stress of the whole day had got to me. I got to the wards and as usual the lifts were reluctant to work, so I climbed the four flights of stairs, virtually on my hands and knees. As usual with new mothers, Eileen was bored and wanted to go home. Happy days!

I went to see my GP the next day and told him that I was supposed to be the happiest man in the world, but with so much pain in my joints, I was so depressed. I sobbed, probably for the best, as it seemed to wash away all the problems and I felt better immediately. The doctor understood my feelings and gave me the support I needed. That was a turning point in my life inasmuch that I would never get stressed again from work related pressure. The job was a means of income, when I left the office, work was instantly forgotten.

To give Eileen a break, I would take Clare in her pram up to Stoke Heath, for an hour or so, and walk around the pitches watching the football matches. I didn't miss playing, the Arthritis had killed the enthusiasm, but I wasn't a very good spectator either. Besides, I had a new baby now, and hopefully I would share more of my time with her, than I did with Wendy, when football was my priority.

Part 2 Meet the Teams
Teams that I played for, during the 1960's and 70's and the League positions they achieved.

Season	Saturday League	Sunday League
1963/64	Moseley United	-
1964/65	Moseley United	-
1965/66	Moseley United	-
1966/67	Moseley United	-
1967/68	Moseley United	AC Godiva
1968/69	Moseley United	AC Godiva
1969/70	Moseley United	Parkstone WMC
1970/71	Avondale	Parkstone WMC
1971/72	Avondale	-
1972/73	Avondale	Barras Green Rangers
1973/74	-	Barras Green WMC
1974/75	Barras Green Rangers	Barras Green WMC
1976/77	Barras Green Rangers	Barras WMC/ Apollo Rgrs.
1975/76	-	Apollo Rangers
1977/78	-	Apollo Rangers
1978/79	-	Colliers FC

Moseley United
Coventry and District (Saturday) League.

Season	Div'n	Pos'n	P	W	D	L	F	A	Pts
1963/64	1	12th of 12	22	3	2	17	30	105	8
1964/65	2	1st of 12	22	17	2	3	94	37	36
1965/66	1	9th of 12	22	8	4	10	58	52	20
1966/67	1	7th of 13	24	11	2	11	58	39	24
1967/68	1	11th of 13	24	6	3	15	39	52	15
1968/69	1	9th of 13	24	7	9	8	35	42	23
1969/70	1	6th of 11	20	8	2	10	38	57	18

Moseley United Reserves
Coventry and District (Saturday) League

Season	Div'n	Pos'n	P	W	D	L	F	A	Pts
1963/64	Junior	11th of 14	26	8	3	15	61	90	19
1964/65	Junior	4th of 11	20	10	3	7	59	51	23
1965/66	Sect A	5th of 13	24	11	4	9	70	50	26
1966/67	Sect A	6th of 14	26	12	6	8	67	63	30
1967/68	Sect A	10th of 10	18	2	5	11	29	59	9
1968/69	Sect A	7th of 12	22	9	3	10	46	51	21
1969/70	Sect A	10th of 10	18	0	1	17	15	108	1

A C Godiva
Coventry and District (Sunday) League

Season	Div'n	Pos'n	P	W	D	L	F	A	Pts
1967/68	3	3rd of 9	16	8	4	4	41	23	20
1968/69	2	5th of 10	18	9	2	7	43	43	20

Avondale FC
Coventry and District (Saturday) League

Season	Div'n	Pos'n	P	W	D	L	F	A	Pts
1970/71	Sect A	2nd of 10	20	15	3	2	84	33	33
1971/72	2	3rd of 15	28	18	4	6	72	45	40
1972/73	2	1st of 14	26	17	5	4	85	36	39

Parkstone 'A'
Coventry and District (Sunday) League

Season	Div'n	Pos'n	P	W	D	L	F	A	Pts
1969/70	Sen'r 1	2nd of 11	20	15	3	2	80	24	33
1970/71	Prem 2	5th of 9	16	6	3	7	34	42	15

Parkstone 'B'
Coventry and District (Sunday) League

Season	Div'n	Pos'n	P	W	D	L	F	A	Pts
1969/70	Sen'r 2	4th of 12	22	10	4	8	69	43	24
1970/71	Sen'r 2	1st of 12	22	18	2	2	110	44	38

Barras Green Rangers
Coventry and District (Sunday) League 1972/73 only
Coventry and District (Saturday) League

Season	Div'n	Pos'n	P	W	D	L	F	A	Pts
1972/73	Sen'r 5	5th of 12	22	13	2	7	92	42	28
1974/75	Sect B	2nd of 10	18	14	2	2	107	23	30
1975/76	Sect A	1st of 12	22	21	1	0	106	21	43

Barras Green WMC
Coventry and Central Warwickshire (Sunday) League

Season	Div'n	Pos'n	P	W	D	L	F	A	Pts
1973/74	Sen'r 2	1st of 10	18	14	3	1	99	26	31
1974/75	Sen'r 1	1st of 10	16	15	0	1	94	23	30
1975/76	Prem 2	1st of 10	18	15	1	2	84	33	31

Apollo Rangers/ Colliers FC
Coventry and District (Sunday) League

Season	Div'n	Pos'n	P	W	D	L	F	A	Pts
1975/76	Sen'r 4	7th of 12	18	7	4	11	37	42	18
1976/77	Sen'r 4	4th of 12	22	13	3	6	72	34	29
1977/78	Sen'r 4	4th of 12	21	11	5	5	61	64	27
1978/79	Sen'r 3	7th of 11	19	8	1	10	52	68	17

Moseley United FC.
Moseley United Reserves.
Moseley United Colts (later renamed Doubleday FC)

I have been able to find league tables dating back to 1951 for Moseley United's first team, and 1952 for the reserve team. Both teams started in the Coventry and District League Junior Division. I can only assume that the football club was started by a group of workers who lived in the Coundon and Radford areas of the city, and were probably employed at the nearby factories of Daimler and Alvis.

I first played for Moseley United in September 1963. Reg Kimber, the Secretary of the club, worked at Wickman, and convinced me that I would enjoy my football in the Coventry and District League, rather than the Works League.

Moseley still ran two teams, the First team was in Division 1, and the Reserve team in Junior Division. Apparently, the First team had survived relegation, by good fortune and due to other clubs folding. There had been an influx of younger players during the previous season, and the club was optimistic of better times!

I was pleased to get my chance in the Reserves immediately. My debut game was a cup match at Fillongley. At that time, it was usual to meet at Wheatley Street prior to away games. Home games were on parks pitches (usually the Memorial Park). Not everyone had transport, and Reg took me to Fillongley on his scooter, a bit different to my push bike! We arrived safely, and the match was played on a "ridge and furrow" field. This dates back to the middle ages, when fields were always ploughed in the same direction, resulting in a pattern of parallel ridges and troughs. It made running and ball control difficult at times.

The game was very even, and although we lost 1-0, I thought that the team played well, and I was pleased with my game. The home team provided a cup of tea after the game, which I thought was nice, and friendly. I can't remember getting a cup of anything elsewhere!

Moseley United held weekly meetings at the Stag Inn, at the corner of Bishop Street and Lamb Street. The idea was to talk about the previous weekend's matches, and select the teams for the forthcoming games, as well as any other business. It was a good opportunity to get to know my new teammates and members of the First team.

The First team played in blue shirts and white shorts and socks, and the second team in tangerine shirts and white shorts and socks. The next Reserve game was a Telegraph Cup fixture at home, on the Memorial park. There were a few different faces in our team, but the opposition, Baginton British Legion Reserves, were better than us and won 4-2. The next weekend we would play them again in a league match at their ground in Bubbenhall village.

John Colledge was keen to play, and he came to the next meeting. The Reserve team was always struggling for players and John was selected to play, along with some "retired" players, who were drafted in. We drew 3-3 in a much improved performance, and I scored my first goal. John made a lasting impression on several of the opponents, and one of the "retired" players Ken Hopkins, who was around forty at the time, raced around the pitch like a ten year old. What an example to the younger players! Ken's favourite saying was "you can't put an old head on young shoulders"

John and I were not the only youngsters at the club, in fact we frequently had a forward line of seventeen year olds. The older players generally played at the back and offered advice, but I can't ever remember tactics being discussed. It was up to the players in the team to play to the best of their ability and adapt their skills to suit their team.

The season progressed and both teams struggled to get a win. The First team got hammered in some matches, losing 9-0 to Hastings United, and 10-4 in the return game, and 12-0 to Fillongley. The Reserves didn't concede so many goals; the only bad results were against Sherwyn Albion 8-2, and Brassworkers who beat us 5-0 and 7-4 on their way to the league title.

It was mid January before the First team won a match and then another, beating Tile Hill Old Boys 2-1 and Baginton BL 3-2. A 4-2 win against St. Lukes completed the season's victories. John, who was a first team regular by now, was particularly pleased with the win at

Smorral Lane, Exhall against St. Lukes, not only did he score two goals, but it 'wiped the smirk off the face' of an opposing player. The team finished bottom of the division with 8 points, and was relegated to Division Two. In Cup competitions they managed to win the first round tie in the Boyd Carpenter Cup, beating Christ Church 9-0, who played in Division 1 of the Coventry and Surburban League.

The Reserves finished fourth from bottom of the Junior Division with 19 points, just above Whoberley Wanderers Reserves, and Avondale FC (who were in their first season), and Brinklow who managed just four points.

It was a disappointing climax for both teams, because there were some good players in the club, unfortunately they never managed to get a run of wins under the belt, to give the players more confidence. I had enjoyed my first season and was looking forward to the next.

When Baginton BL folded, Moseley took over the use of the pitch at Bubbenhall, and used it for several years, until the local villagers raised a football team. The Parish Council then gave them priority of use. We would use the village "Reading rooms" as changing rooms. The property was a double fronted house, which was used as the local community centre. An elderly couple lived in the rear section of the house, and provided a caretaker service. They would tidy and clean the rooms after we had left. They were lovely people and we always treated them respectfully.

The football pitch was on the village playing fields and we shared the use with a Sunday league side, Molloy Athletic. On rare occasions, we would have to make quick repairs to the goalposts after they had been damaged during the week. On one occasion, one of the vertical posts had been lifted out of its socket and left lying on the ground, damaging the crossbar attachment. We managed to raise the post and tried to put it into the socket, but the vandals had filled the socket with bricks and stones. The referee was quite patient, and we managed to clear some of the rubble, but the post was sitting about a foot too high. We proceeded to play the game, and the referee told us that he would use his discretion in the event that a goal was scored in the high part of the goal. At the end of the game he hadn't been called upon to make that decision.

Replacement goal posts were not readily available, and the response to the vandalism was to replace the wooden goalposts with steel tube welded set. These were damaged, when the local Tarzan swung on the crossbar and bent it. The problems subsided, when the vandalism was raised at the local parish council meeting.

The grass was cut quite regularly by one of the local farmers, but the goal areas suffered from continual use during the summer, and the parish council would arrange for their gardeners to reseed the bare patches. It was left to the teams that rented the pitch to mark out the touchlines and penalty areas etc. When I took over as club secretary, I appealed for assistance in marking the pitch at the start of the season.

We had a roller machine stored at the playing field, all that was needed was some creosote, and a few keen players to get there about an hour or two early to do the job. The touchlines and penalty areas, were to a certain extent, still visible through the new growth of grass, so measuring and pegging out string wasn't required. Guess who was still pushing the machine around the pitch, when it was time to kick off the match? Thanks for the help chaps!

Now that Moseley United's home games were at Bubbenhall, the meeting point for players prior to the game, was changed from Wheatley Street to The Plough Inn on the corner of London Road and Gulson Road, which was better for parking, and gave us a clear run down to Ryton and onto Bubbenhall. The Plough offered the chance of some socialising before the game, and the alcohol would give us an edge in our game.

I loved playing football at Bubbenhall, it is a pretty little village off the Ryton to Leamington road. The playing field is situated at the lower end of the village, and gives good views over the fields toward Coventry and the river Avon valley. Bubbenhall had a large pitch, and I was able to use that space in my game, as I favoured the long ball, and my trusty left boot could measure a decent pass. We had some quick players up front, and I could change defence into attack with a forty yard pass.

The football team members change from year to year, and so therefore does the team's strengths and abilities. When I joined Moseley United there was a good mix of youth and experience. Alan Setchell, Steve Whitmore, Stan Bradley and Robert Lindop were the better young players who had established themselves in the First team, playing alongside the experience of Bert Ottley, Pete Webb, Pete Lewis and goalkeeper Derek Langford. Recent arrivals of the two Johns, Crudginton and Sanders, and Pat Mahon would bolster the defence, and the sharpness of Pete Janes, Jimmy Farquhar and Ben Vallely up front would enable the First team to regain their position in Division 1 in the Coventry and District League.

The Reserve team had a backbone of stalwart players. These are the older players who have played for the club for many years, and have lost their sharpness through age and/or injury. Their knowledge of the game is more important to the seventeen year old, than their skills. It was a pleasure to play alongside Ken Hopkins, Colin Swift, Gordon Bradley and Jack Gill.

The second string team selection is always going to be fluid, the priority is to put out your strongest side in the First team. Without injuries it is possible to get a settled Reserve team. There was a flush of new young players joined the club after John and I started playing.
Fred West, Pete Hewitt, Ian Hart, Dave Sephton, Larry Watson, Ricky Bevan, Mick Harrington and Vince McTavish all competed for selection alongside regulars Reg New, Reg Kimber, Colin Swift, Ken and Mick Hopkins, little Jimmy Henry, and goalkeeper Alan Freeman.

Larry Watson was a character. We first met him at the Memorial Park where he was offering his services to teams short of players. He was already changed into his shorts and boots and said he could play in goal and on the wing. We needed a player and signed him. It was alright to use a new player as long as the opposition didn't object and the Referee sanctioned it. Larry was a good asset for the club, and would play for several years before training to be a Referee.

He was a goal scorer and when in goal an excellent keeper. His attitude was right and he hardly ever complained. He turned up on time, kit on, played the game, and was gone within minutes of the game ending. He obviously lived life to the full. When he qualified to be a Referee, he was eager to progress to Class 1 standard in the shortest period of time, and could be seen refereeing several games over the weekend. He was always available.

We met later, when he refereed a game at Caludon Park, I wasn't particularly happy with some of his decisions during the game. He had pulled me up for a foul inside the opponent's penalty area, the goalkeeper put the ball down inside the box and side footed it forward. His team members were expecting a long goal kick and had their back to him, as did Larry. I saw an advantage the ball came out of the area, and I ran in and smacked the ball into the net. The goalkeeper was moaning that the free kick was outside the box, and Larry confirmed it, and booked me. Well, I hit the roof! I think he knew he was in the wrong, otherwise he would have sent me off for the abuse I gave him. Not one of my better days. Larry was a successful Referee and did eventually run the line at a FA Cup final

The Reserve team played in the Junior Division (later known as Section A) of the Coventry and District League. It is good for the football club to have more players than it needs to fill in the team sheet, but if the players can't get a game, then they will go elsewhere. There was times when Moseley couldn't field a full team, but they were no different to many other clubs in the league.

The 1964/65 season was to be a good one for the club, the First team would win the Second Division title and the Reserves would finish fourth in their Division. The First teams' success was down to the clinical finishing of Jimmy Farquhar, who scored 38 goals, with good back up from Stan Bradley, Peter Janes, Steve Whitmore and Alan Setchell. The team won 17 out of 22 league games, drew 2 and losing 3, title challengers Howitzers and Meriden Rovers inflicting defeats.

The Reserve team won their first three games and promptly lost the next three to the teams that would be fighting for the title, Meadway Rovers Reserves and Queen Margaret's. There were good wins against Veasey and Sharples (8-2) and Sherwyn Albion Reserves (9-1), which included a rare goal from full back Reg Kimber. Pete Hewitt and Larry Watson were scoring freely.

The return game against Queen Margaret's was riotous, there was no official referee, and one of the Queen Margaret's supporters took on the onerous task. However, the first half went without incident and in a competitive game Moseley were 2-1 up at half time. It was clear to us that something had been arranged between the visiting team and 'their referee'. The number of decisions going the way of Queen Margaret's caused a lot of anger, confrontation and reckless tackles. We lost 7-2, several goals resulting from dubious refereeing. This was the first time that I had seen such menace on a football pitch – not pleasant.

The weather was good during the season, and the Reserve team had to play in a Supplementary Cup from the beginning of March, fortunately, we didn't have to play Queen Margaret's again. The division was split into two groups of five teams. We played four games on a mini league basis, the winners of group A met the winners of group B. We won 2, drew 1, and lost 1, not good enough to qualify for the final.

When Coventry City Football Club opened there new training facility at Ryton, local leagues were asked to enter under18's teams to play in a knock out competition to be played on their all weather pitches under floodlights. The Coventry and District League asked all teams to submit two or three names, from which they would select a team to play in the competition.

My name came out of the hat, and the "team" had to turn up at Highfield Road on the specified date. We changed in the CCFC first team dressing rooms. Our kit was provided by the League, a bit dated, but the shirts were red and green halves, as shown on the City of Coventry Crest.

We were ferried by coach to Ryton to play the match, only to find that the pitch was shale, not grass. We weren't sure who we were playing against, a Nuneaton or a Leamington League team, and nobody, except the goalkeeper, knew what position to play! It wasn't a pleasant night it was cold and wet, and after a kick about it was obvious that the pitch was dangerous, you only had to kneel down to tie your boot laces, and your knee would be bleeding. We played the game, but no-one had experience at that time, of playing under lights, on those pitches, and were still trying to do slide tackles. The opposition adapted better than us and won easily. Our goalkeeper was masked in blood and crushed shale. We went back to Highfield Road on the coach, God knows what the driver thought when he went to clean his coach!

The staff at Highfield Road, were amazed at the bloodletting and had to call for more assistance. I was fortunate, I escaped with grazes on knees and hands only. We were told that we had played in the first football match to be played at Ryton on those pitches. A painful piece of history!

1965/66 Season and the return to the First Division started quite well for the First team with 4 wins and a draw, there was some close games, and a win (9-2) against Balsall & Berkswell. We would later beat them 10-2, (they lost all their league matches conceding 129 goals in 22 games). We then went through a bad spell, losing four on the trot. The worst defeat was to Stoke Aldermoor (1-6).

The difference this season was that it was harder to score against better sides, and our defence was quite leaky, and yet I thought we had better players than two years before.

I always enjoyed games against Stoke Aldermoor, Meriden Rovers and Meadway Rovers. The away match at Folly Lane gave me some satisfaction. I had always wanted to play on the pitches at London Road, having passed them umpteen times on the way to Bubbenhall. I didn't realise that 'the Lane's' pitch was actually at the rear of the dressing rooms on the other side of the road! I had a good game that day, even though I say it myself, and although we lost, I scored our goal in the 3-1 defeat.

In the game against the Howitzers, captain and full back, Bert Ottley, broke a leg. The team were already without four regular players due to injury, but were leading 2-1 at the time of the accident. Moseley dug deep and Alan Setchell scored two goals before half time. Howitzers fought back and squared the game at 4-4, before Stan Bradley made the game safe with a two goal burst.

The League had expanded to five divisions, the Junior Division was renamed Section A, and the new Division was Section B. The Reserves had a good season considering, finishing fifth out of thirteen teams in the division, winning more games than they lost. Their heaviest defeat was at the hands of Brassworkers Reserves who finished below us in the division. Whexford United was a new team in the Division, the name baffled plenty of people, until it was explained. The team members came from three churches at Wheelwright Lane, Exhall and Radford. I knew one of their team from Foxford School, Taff Davies, once seen, never forgotten! Taff was a big lad, strong and a good footballer, and he always had a smile on his face. At that time Welsh people in England were as rare as Indians and Pakistanis. I only knew two Welshmen, Taff, and Bob Pinkett, (Dunlop Apprentice) who was at Coventry Technical College and Lanchester College with me.

The 1966/67 season started with a bang for both teams, the First team won 4 and drew 1, completing the double over Howitzers 8-2 and 10-1 and beating Fillongley 2-0, and Saunders Hall 5-0, before drawing 3-3 with Clarksons Sports. Clarksons would go on to win the Division 1 title at the first attempt. The initial burst couldn't be maintained and a post Christmas slump of four defeats, all by the odd goal, put paid to title hopes as those defeats were against teams that would finish behind Clarksons. However, the rest of the season was generally even, but the final position in the table could have been better, if the last four games had not been defeats, Meadway Rovers and Unicorn Celtic completing doubles. We played 24 games winning and losing 11 and drawing 2. The pleasing thing was that the 'goals for' total was much more that the 'goals against' 58-39. Final position was seventh out of thirteen.

The Reserves good start was against weaker sides. Whexford United, Rayon Rangers, Unicorn Celtic Reserves and St James soon put us in our place, but the encouraging sign was that the defeats were not by more than two goals. That is until we played Barras Green twice in a fortnight, losing 9-0 and 2-0. The return against Rayon Rangers was a 7-2 defeat, and we also lost to Unicorn Celtic Reserves again 4-3. In March/April we won four league matches which consolidated our League position! We finished sixth out of fourteen, and won 12, drew 6, and lost 8. The 'goals for' total was 67, and the 'goals against' 63.

The 1967/68 season started with renewed confidence and expectation. The dream was shattered early on when both teams failed to win a game in September. The First team drew one of five games losing the others by the odd goal, and the Reserves lost three and drew two. One game, against YCW Reserves, resulted in a 0-5 defeat. It would not count, as later on in the season YCW resigned, and their records were deleted.

Throughout the season the First team continued to scrap for points, losing many games by the odd goal, only Ryton United beat us comfortably 1-4. We managed 6 wins, including a 5-1 win over St. Lukes, drew 3, and lost 15 of the 24 matches, finishing eleventh out of thirteen. Goals for was 39 and 52 against.

The Reserves won only two games; 2-1 against Henley College and 6-0 against Leofric United. In that game Ben Vallely scored five of the goals, and Bert Ottley made his first appearance since breaking his leg. Heaviest defeats were against Baginton British Legion who won 7-1 in both matches. The final table read played 18, won 2, drew 5, lost 11, for 29 against 59 points 9. No guesses for who was bottom of the division!

Reg Kimber, the club secretary, introduced two young lads, Steve Twigg and Mick Boston, who were in their final year at Whitley Abbey School. They played in the school football team and were keen to play in the adult league. They were given the opportunity to shine in the Reserve team, and slotted in well. Their mates soon wanted to play also, and to satisfy all of them, Moseley United Colts was formed. Initially, because it was mid-season, the new team could only play friendly matches against league teams, who had a free Saturday.

Despite the Reserve team finishing bottom of the Section A, the introduction of Moseley United Colts into the Section B gave the Reserves a stay of execution, and for the 1968/69 season they would play in Section A again.

The First team survived again, out 24 games they won 7, drew 9, and lost 8. The goals for (35) and against (42) told the story of their season – need a striker, tight defence. The weather was bad that season and many games were postponed during January, February and March, resulting in the season being extended and evening matches. This plays havoc with acquiring results from the Coventry Evening Telegraph Pink Edition, and is therefore difficult for me to present an assessment of the Club's performance this season. From the results that are available, only Leamington Celtic, the eventual Division 1 champions, beat us easily (0-6).

The Reserve team had a better season, probably due to the new lads, finishing seventh of twelve teams, with 9 wins, 3 draws, and 10 losses. The goals tally of 46 for and 51 against was similar to the First team. Heaviest defeats were 1-7 to Stoke Aldermoor Reserves and 0-5 against Avondale.

The Colts team took some time to settle in to playing junior football, losing three of the first five league games. To their credit they learnt fast and won the next eight fixtures, inflicting some heavy results, Keresley Celtic suffering the worst, losing 15-0 and 7-0. The Colts would finish third out of ten teams, winning 12, and losing 6, scoring 99 goals and conceding 39.

Reg had entered the team in the Birmingham County FA Youth Cup and they were very successful in reaching the final. Tragedy was to strike down one of the players in a road traffic accident.

Brian Doubleday had to have a leg amputated as a result of the collision. The team played the final soon after, losing 4-3 in a close tie, and immediately after visited Brian in hospital. After the final, the bond of the young team was even stronger, and several fund raising schemes were arranged to help Brian to cope better with his disability. He would make a swift recovery, and was soon up and about and helping in team affairs, assisting Reg Kimber.

The Colts players were close knit and were happier playing in the Colts team rather than their better players being seconded into the Reserve and First teams. To avoid friction with the Moseley committee, the Colts team decided to go it alone, changing the name of the team to Doubleday FC. They had been self-financing since inauguration, and had nothing to lose, but everything to gain!

Unfortunately, for Moseley United, they lost the best Secretary in the League. Reg Kimber was the driving force of the club, and his enthusiasm and dedication was to be sorely missed. I have had a good relationship with Reg ever since my first days at Wickman, and he was the Company representative at the Council House, when I was made a Freeman of the City of Coventry. As well as his interest in football, he was Secretary of the Wickman Railway Club (disbanded recently), and the Secretary of the Whitley Local History Group.

It was the start of the 1969/70 season and I took over as Secretary of Moseley United FC, and did it for a season. I had a good idea of what was required, and Reg was on hand at work to advise me. Everything was fine until the weather caught me out!

The weather had been terrible since Christmas and it had led to a serious backlog of fixtures. There had been continuous rain, snow, ice and frosts for most of January, February and March and the parks pitches in Coventry and the surrounding villages were unplayable. It wasn't a case of which games were off; it was which games are on. Notices were put in the Coventry Evening Telegraph to confirm that parks pitches in Coventry, Nuneaton and Leamington areas were unplayable. One week, both Moseley teams had away games in the Leamington area. The First team were playing Whitnash, at Radford Semele, just outside of Leamington, and the Reserves playing Leamington Celtic. I had been to work on the Saturday morning and Mum said that a man had rung from Leamington to say that the game was off. I took it to be the Radford Semele match, knowing that the parks pitches were off. In hindsight, I should have rung the chap back! We met as usual, at the Plough on London Road, and only the first team players turned up. I told them that the game was off, and we all went home, after a pint or two in the pub.

I was a bit surprised to have a phone call from the League Match Secretary, asking why we hadn't turned up for the match at Radford Semele, adding that the pitch was playable, and the opposition and the referee were changed ready to play. I told him that with all the postponements in recent weeks, I was surprised that any games would be played. He wasn't happy; he already had hundreds of games to reschedule.

I had to attend a disciplinary meeting and explain my actions, or lack of them, to the Committee. I was reprimanded, and told to reimburse the expenses of the referee, and the Whitnash FC, as well as a small fine to cover League administration. Altogether, just over six pound fine. That didn't go down well at the production of Moseley's balance sheet at the Annual General Meeting. The club members thought that I should pay the fine! Well sorry, but we're all in it together chaps!

It was business as usual for the First team this season. Again the football program was ravaged by the weather during January, February and March. Leamington Celtic won the Division 1 title again doing the double over us 1-9 and 1-3. The team managed to finish sixth out of eleven, winning 8, drawing 2 and losing 10. The need for a consistent striker, and tighter defence, was once again highlighted with 38 goals for and 57 against. The Moseley United v Hen Lane Social match in December was the Star Junior Match of the Day in the CET Pink Edition. Read it in 'Press Reports'

The Reserves had a miserable season, finished bottom of Section A, and would be relegated. The team failed to win a game, and only drew 1, losing the rest, scoring only 15 goals and conceding 108! Heaviest defeat was 0-16 to Hen Lane Social Reserves. Leamington Celtic Reserves took pity on us by drawing one goal each.

Doubleday on the other hand, came top of Section B and won promotion! Winning all but one match, the team scored 126 goals and only let in15.The game they lost was to Unbrako 0-1, Doubleday won the return 3-0. Incredibly Unbrako had identical results. The title was decided on 'goal average', not goal difference as it is today. Well done boys!

The position of Secretary was vacant, because I had already decided to leave Moseley United and play for Avondale FC. None of the current players wanted the job. A young lad who had only joined the club recently, attended the meeting with his mate. The poor chap had only come along for a drink, but walked out the door as Honorary Secretary, with all of the club's records and accounts etc. I was stunned!

Despite all of this, I was proud to have played for a club that had been in existence for nearly twenty years, at the time of my exit. It is quite a feat, for an amateur football club to survive without sponsorship and outside funding.

The football club continued despite relegation of both teams to lower divisions, and eventually the reserve team folded at the end of the 1972/73 season, after failing to win a match and conceding 136 goals in 30 games. The first team battled on, and they transferred to the Coventry Combination for the 1974/75 season, where they had some success reaching the final of the Hubert Cup, losing to Wycliffe and winning the title in the 1975/76 season. The club folded at the end of the 1976/77 season.

Doubleday FC was very successful and gained three promotions before leaving the District League to join the Coventry and North Warwickshire League in 1972/73 season where they played in the Premier division. They then transferred to the Coventry Combination for the 1974/75 season. The club folded at the end of the 1976/77 season.

It was perhaps ironic, that Moseley United and Doubleday FC should be playing in the same League when they both met their demise.

AC Godiva (formerly George Hudson FC)

George Hudson FC was founded in 1963. It was one of the founder members of the Coventry and District Sunday League Junior Division. They changed the name of the club to AC Godiva in October 1966. The original name was inappropriate when George Hudson was sold by CCFC. The team meetings were being held at the Godiva pub, (now Rosie Malone's) in Jordan Well, and it was no surprise that the name of the football club should follow the name of the hostelry.

When Sunday football took off in the early 1960's there was a couple of teams that took the names of their clubs from their professional hero's at Coventry City FC, at the start of the Sky Blue revolution led by Jimmy Hill. The teams were George Hudson FC and Machin Athletic. The professional was made club president and no doubt it was expected that he would pass on a few tips to the eager amateurs, and probably donate a set of kit and a couple of footballs!

Ernie Machin was one of those players, whose name was put on the team sheet first. He played for CCFC for ten years from 1962, and made over two hundred and fifty first team appearances. He was a midfield dynamo and scored thirty five goals in a career that was restricted by knee injuries and a car crash.

George Hudson was an ace centre forward, who came from Peterborough United to replace Terry Bly, a crowd favourite and prolific goal scorer, twenty five in thirty two appearances. The difference between the players was as chalk and cheese. Bly, who also came from Peterborough, was not a skilful player but had plenty of hustle and bustle, and a thunderous right boot. Hudson was a cultered player, who read the game well and instantly won over the Coventry faithful with a hat-trick on his debut, and went onto score seventy five goals in one hundred and twenty nine appearances.

When George Hudson FC played one of their first matches at Coundon Hall Park, I went with John Colledge to watch the game, and stood next to George Hudson himself. I was surprised that I was taller than he was. He stayed till half time, probably because his team was leaking goals. John's interest in the game was more to do with the fact that Hudson's players were his ex-schoolmates from Whitley Abbey.

George Hudson was transferred three years later much to the disgust of the fans. The club continued, although never setting the world alight.

John and I started playing for AC Godiva in the 1967/68 season. The club played their home matches at Prior Deram Walk, Canley. The pitches were fairly flat but could get waterlogged easily. The team played in dark blue shirts, shorts and socks. The manager was Graham Lissaman, and the team played a 4-3-3 system; probably not planned, but it worked. The goalkeeper was Alf Betts, and the back four was John Gair, Rod West, captain Mick Ansell and Trevor Long. John and Trevor, on the flanks, were good tacklers and weren't afraid to put their boot through the ball. Rod was a short stocky chap, who could out jump most six foot centre forwards, amazing! Mick Ansell was the best captain that I ever played with, he led by example, and marshalled the defence admirably, and he was a good no nonsense footballer. The midfield was dominated by Rob Gaulden and John Donnelly, both skilful players who would run all day long with the ball at their feet. They were ably assisted by John Colledge who added the necessary bite, and Graham Smith who filled in the gaps and threaded the ball through to the front men. I played up front on the left, with Ray Munday in the middle, and industrious Bobby Caves on the right. Bob Hancox was the Mr Reliable always available, and the regular substitute; who slotted into any position if there was an absentee on a Sunday morning. Manager Graham Lissaman would also play if required.

The team played in the Coventry and District Sunday League - Senior Division 3, and in the first of the two seasons that I would play for them, was quite successful, and challenged for the top places in the Division. Unfortunately, we couldn't beat the two teams that finished above us in the Division, Coventry Railwaymen's Club and Colwyn Villa. That season we only played sixteen league games, due to Keresley Bell being expelled from the league, but we won 8 drew 4 and lost 4, scoring 41 goals and conceding 23. Highest win was 7-0 against Rugby Medina who finished bottom but one. In the various Cup competitions, we had good wins against Eaves and Washbourne (7-0) and Stoneleigh (7-2), but lost two matches against Division 1 opposition Poplar Athletic (6-2) and Lime Tree Park (4-0). In all matches AC Godiva was never outplayed.

At the commencement of the 1968/69 season AC Godiva was to play in the Senior League Division 2. It was not a promotion as such more a rearrangement of the whole league. We started off badly; losing three of the first four matches, one of the games was against Courtiers (0-4); we would later get our revenge thrashing them 10-1. Courtiers would finish bottom of the table.

The next game was against Coventry Railwayman's Club at Prior Deram Walk. It was at that time a top of the table clash, and there was good support for both teams on the touchline. We played good football and were on top throughout, the 4-3-3 system working to perfection.

We won 6-1 and our supporters got louder as the goals went in. I scored the sixth chasing down a backpass by the opposing defender, it was under hit and the goalkeeper didn't have time to collect the ball. I won the ball in the tackle, and it spun towards the goal, as I ran into score, the supporters gave a crescendo of cheers, just like the crowd at professional matches jeer the opposing keeper when he takes a goal kick.

The second season wasn't as successful and instead of winning against teams we had beaten previously, we were losing. Machin Athletic beat us 7-0 and there was quite a lot of grumbling after. The match had been a battle at times and there was quite a lot of bad tackles. I gave one penalty away when I chopped someone down in the area. It wasn't clever, but I was frustrated by the lack of aggression from my team mates. Machin were hitting us hard, and it seemed that only me and John were giving as good as we got. Our foul play didn't go down well with Captain Mick on the day, but he didn't bear a grudge, and it was back to normal the next week.

The heaviest defeat was 11-0 against Phoenix Royal, who we had beaten 4-1 earlier in the season. (We only had nine players). The final league table showed us in fifth position, winning 9 drawing 2 and losing 7. Perhaps the best result was against Youell Athletic, who would go on to win the title; we lost to them 1-0 in the first game of the season, but reversed the score line later to end Youell's unbeaten record!

Travelling to home games was difficult on a Sunday morning. Not many younger people had cars then, and the main mode of transport was the bus, or bike. To ride over to Canley play a game of football, and the cycle back, was an effort to say the least. The buses, on a Sunday morning, were as not as regular as Haley's Comet, and you had to catch two, there was no direct service.

John had passed his driving test, soon after his 18th birthday, and also enjoyed a beer or two. In those days, you could drink and drive, John was a capable driver and knew his limit, or said he did! His brother, Mick, was serving in the Army in Aden, and when Mick was home on leave John would spend time with him, mainly in the Old Hall in Lythall's Lane. Football was on hold!

Occasionally, Graham Lissaman would offer me a lift, but he usually had a car full. I decided to quit the club and play for Parkstone Working Men's Club, whose home games were local on Longford Park, and they provided transport to away matches.

I felt that AC Godiva would continue to be a successful club, but the Coventry and District Sunday League again rearranged the league set up and put AC Godiva in Division 1 of the Senior League. That was in effect two promotions in two years for finishing 3rd out of 9, and 5th out of 10.

The rearrangement would not help AC Godiva. The team obviously did not manage to attract good players, and whilst they completed their 1969/70 League program, they finished bottom of Division 1, losing all twenty matches. They managed to score on average one goal a game, but unfortunately the goals against totalled 116. It was no surprise that the team did not feature again. By coincidence, Machin Athletic did not feature that season, although they may have changed the name of the team.

I enjoyed my two seasons with the lads of AC Godiva, we played good football, and impressed many people, but in hindsight you cannot run a team with just thirteen or fourteen players. I felt for manager Graham Lissaman at times, I don't know how he kept a head of hair!

If you read the article about the beginnings of the Coventry and District Sunday League, you may understand why they had to take the decisions that they did. The League was only formed five years before, and due to the popularity with Sunday football, the expansion was overwhelming. In the words of Ex-Match Secretary Vic Terry, "It was like Topsy, it just grew and grew!" (Topsy was a character in the book 'Uncle Tom's Cabin' by Harriet Beecher Stowe).

Parkstone WMC Football Club
Founded 1963

Parkstone WMC Football Club ran two teams in the Coventry and District Sunday League. The home games were mostly played at Longford Park. The park had been upgraded, and four new football pitches provided, and new dressing rooms built. The success of the Sunday game in local amateur football meant that parks pitches were now at a premium.

My brother Roger was playing for the 'A' team. They played in the Division 1 of the League, and had some class players. The 'B' team played in Division 4, and the team sheets could change, dependant on injuries received the previous day, or the volume of ale the previous night!

My time with Parkstone wasn't very memorable; I helped out with the normal pre-match hassle of team changes, kit, corner flags, bucket and sponge, oranges, Referees etc. Either I wasn't selected or I was the substitute who didn't get the chance to get on the pitch.

It had to change, I got on as a substitute at half time when we were playing in a Cup tie against Dunchurch, who were in the Premier League Division 2. It was a glorious day, and we were playing on a good pitch, unfortunately we were soon 3-0 down. I felt good and played up front, and chased the ball and harried the opposing defenders.

The rest of my team seemed to pick up on my efforts and we ended the game 5-4 winners, Graham Fletcher scoring a hat-trick.

I managed to get a few games during the rest of the season playing on the left wing, possibly because no one else wanted the job. The next season, and I was now a regular in the 'B' team, and later in the season made the 'A' team, who were pushing for the league title. I managed to score a couple of goals and make a few, but it all came down to the final game of the season against Dolphin Athletic. The match was attended by a few hundred Dolphin supporters, and was played on a smallish sloping pitch in a strong wind. The opposition were up for it more than us, and beat us 6-1. I hardly touched the ball in the first half, and had been clobbered a few times. I was eventually substituted early in the second half, much to my relief.

I married Eileen before the next season started. I had my stag night at the Parkstone WM Club, and many of the players turned up, even though it was a Wednesday. They duly saturated my insides with copious cocktails of spirits, and left me wallowing in sick in the toilets. I was told that my legs gave way about thirty yards from home. The next day didn't happen, but I did manage to get to work on the Friday, for another liquid lunch, and a traditional send-off from my workmates.

I remember a couple of goals that I made during my time with Parkstone. The first one was in the 'B' team and I was on the left wing, I had made a run down the touchline and beat a couple of opponents, I cut inside but was forced toward the goal line just outside the penalty area. I managed to look across the area and noticed that the defenders and goalkeeper had come to the near post, and that Graham Fletcher the centre forward had drifted off to the back post. I managed to hook my trusty left foot around and under the ball and float a cross to the far post where Graham outjumped a scrambling defender to head home.

The second was during one my brief appearances in the 'A' team, and it was on my favourite pitch at Longford Park. I wasn't familiar with the opposition, but their goalkeeper was goading our centre forward of the day Gilbert Dobbs, and at some stage he threw the ball direct to Gilly, who smacked it back over the crossbar, more abuse followed. Later, both Gilly and me went for the same through ball. The goalkeeper blocked off Gilly and left me to slot the ball home.

Gilbert was still taking a ribbing, but we shut the keeper up, when I ran down the wing and sent in a fast curling cross, Gilly didn't have to change stride and sent a bullet header into the net from just inside the penalty area.

The 'A' Team finshed second in their divison, winning 15 of the 20 matches, scoring 80 goals and conceding 24. They had easy games against my old team AC Godiva, winning 10-1 and 8-0, and their only defeats were to Dolphin Athletic, the championship winners.

The 'B' Team finished fourth in their division, winning 10 of the 22 matches, scoring 69 goals and conceding 43. They also had easier games, completing the double over Hampton in Arden 7-0 and 12-0. Heaviest defeat was against Spartak 1-8.

The start of the 1970/71 season was a bit of a farce, I started in the first team but hadn't trained properly due to the wedding and moving into the home, and the demands of my new wife. I was not match fit and I was soon back on the touchline with the 'B' team. Soon after Christmas, my new mother-in-law died suddenly, and it was time for me to spend more time at home.

Although I only played for Parkstone for a short while, I played with some good footballers and on the social side, enjoyed their company. My thanks to Tommy Gaut 'B' team manager, Barry Shipton, Pete and Graham Fletcher, Barry Osbourne, John Stevens, Bann Thomas, Nobby Sparkes, Mick Wallace, Brian Bates, Matty Hall, John Ashmore, Derek Weeks and Doug Bryson. Fellow Avondale players Tommy Small and Bob Colley also came to play for Parkstone, and stayed a bit longer.

Graham Fletcher was a goal scoring machine, absolutely brilliant, he must have scored hundreds in his lifetime, he played Saturday and Sundays and played for several clubs in the District and Combination Leagues on Saturdays, Meadway Rovers, Foleshill Athletic, Grange United, Triumph Engineering, Potters Green to name a few.

On Sundays, he was content with playing regularly for the Parkstone 'B' team. In my short time playing for Parkstone, I was amazed at some of the goals he scored and for a tall chap he could outjump defenders easily. Most Sundays he would be the worse for wear from the previous nights boozing, (he wasn't the only one), but he would go out and score three or four goals and make it look easy.

One goal that he scored, I remember as clear as day, we were playing on Pitch 1 at Longford Park, and the opposition wasn't good, but Graham picked up the ball in the centre circle and strode forward, but instead of taking it on further, he kicked the ball from full thirty yards, with such force that it flew straight as a die into the goal. It was still rising when it hit the net! I was alongside Graham, and it seemed to happen in slow motion, the ball never spun or deviated, but the goalkeeper couldn't reach it. Fantastic!

On another occasion, we were playing at Prior Deram Walk, and I had already provided a cross for his first headed goal, and we had a corner, I was on the corner of the box and watched as the defenders tried to cut out Graham. I can't remember who took the corner kick, it may have been Derek Weeks, but as he ran up to take the kick, Graham ran toward him taking the defence with him, then he ran in a circle, losing his markers, and got to the far post just as the ball arrived, Graham had to climb high to head the ball down into the goal.

There are tales of other goals that he has scored; you know the ones that make you wonder how did that go in? The ball has hit his knee, shoulder or backside, or it goes in off the crossbar and both posts. My brother Roger has played against Graham and he and his co-defenders made every effort to stop Graham scoring by any foul means if necessary. The game was into injury time and Graham's team had a corner, two defenders went for the ball and got in each others' way, the ball flew the wrong way hit Graham on his standing leg and went in.

I was relieved that I never had to play against him when he played for Meadway Rovers against Moseley United, I was probably in Reserve team. Phew!

The 1970/71 season for the 'A'team was a consolidation year. Two teams would drop out of the Premier Division 2 and their records were deleted. Out of the 16 matches the team won 6, drew 3 and lost 7, scoring 34 goals and conceding 42.

It was a promotion year for the 'B' team and an historic one too! The team tied with Buncranna Hearts having won 18 matches, drawing 2 and losing 2, and although Parkstone scored 110 and conceded 44 goals, Buncranna scored 105 and conceded 42, giving an identical goal average of 2.5. League officials believed it to be a unique situation! In the final matches of the season Parkstone had overcome Barras Green WMC 6-1, and the Hearts had snatched a late winner in a 5-4 victory over Sporting Club Allesley.

In the March 21st issue of The Pink, they reported that Graham Fletcher had taking his goals tally to 55 goals, and that was with three games left to play! Roy of the Rovers!

Avondale FC
First registered 1963

Avondale FC was one of the original sixteen teams that played in the inaugural competition of the Coventry and District Sunday Football League. It was ideal for a new team to get friendly matches during the season, and as Sunday football started mid season, the opportunity to get some games under the belt was too good to pass, despite the fact that they chose to play on Saturdays, and had applied to the Coventry and District (Saturday) League, which Moseley United played in.

Avondale spent several years in the Coventry and District (Saturday) League in Section 'B', improving year on year. They had a good run in the Invitation Cup reaching the semi-final. They had dominated the game hitting the woodwork four times, but lost 1-0. However, this spurred them on and they were promoted to Section 'A', coming second to Doubleday FC. At the beginning of the 1970/71 season, I joined Avondale FC, a team I had played against several times over the years. Two of their players, Ray Staff and Barry Baker, worked in the offices at Wickman, and we used to chat about our previous weekends' matches. At the end of the last season, I said that I was considering leaving Moseley United. Ray and Barry suggested that I should turn up for pre-season training, and meet the team members. They held club meetings at the Old Dyer's Arms in Spon End, and pre-season training took place on a small grassed area to the side of the Old Butts Stadium at the back of the pub. Ideal!

Pre-season training is as necessary for the amateur footballer, as it is for the professional. There the similarity ends. Exercise in any form needs dedication and if you are not getting paid for training – why bother turning up!

Well, for four months in the summer break your body has relaxed, and your muscles have not been stretched, unless you were lucky enough to kick a ball around a beach. Training usually starts with a run round the park, and then some attempt at physical exercise, such as leg stretches, arm swings, star jumps and push ups. If the team didn't have a coach or a practising sadist, then after ten minutes a kick-about would commence, and the players would split into two teams to get some ball work.

Friendly matches were a good way to improve fitness and also give all players in the club a chance to show off their skills. The parks pitches are generally mown and marked out and the goalposts erected, in mid August. Ideally, it is better to arrange an evening game; this is good for rehydration at the pub afterwards, and tactics can be discussed also.

Avondale also organised training during the season. For a small charge we were able to use the gym at Nicholas Chamberlaine school in Bedworth, or enrol at Henley College for "Football coaching" on the all weather pitch under floodlights. The coach was Ray Bird, a true gentleman, and very knowledgeable about amateur football, he even had a column in "The Pink". He coached the Henley College Sunday League team. The players at Avondale liked his style, and asked him to be their coach during the season, which he agreed to do.

Evening sessions over, it was off to the pub, either the Engine in Bedworth, or the Bell Inn at Bell Green, to talk about the last game, the next game, and select the team. A couple of pints helped keep the throat oiled for long and meaningful discussions.

Avondale FC played their home matches at the Memorial Park, usually on pitches 1 or 2, and got changed in the blue huts that used to be adjacent to the pitches. The huts were big enough for the home team and opponents to change in, but had no lighting or water. Water was available from the Park employees' hut at the end of the block. Both pitches were sloping and dipped slightly more toward the brook that ran through the park. Pitch 3 was at the bottom of the slope and was hardly used as it was always sodden.

Playing on those pitches regularly, gave the home side an advantage, and in three seasons I can't remember losing more than four games. It depended on who won the toss of the coin, but Avondale preferred to kick up the slope in the first half, on the basis that the players were fresher and stronger, and in the second half the opposition would be tiring and weaker kicking up the hill. That's the theory! We also had a lucky orange football!

The team was quite established when I joined, and would be settled for the next three seasons. With this stability the club would be able to progress and improve their league status.

The team comprised, goalkeeper Tony Brown, full backs Rod Larcombe and Barry Baker, and centre half Alan Hancox, forming the backbone of the team. Then Bob Colley, John Bird, John Adams and myself in the engine room. The front line was usually Ken Westgarth or Ray Staff, Ron Osmond and Tommy Small. Squad players, Vic Sanders, Rod Prime, Barry Shipton, Terry Shuttleworth and Grayson Minshaw, were competent cover for injuries, and absentees. In some ways the team picked itself, and the old adage says that "you shouldn't change a winning team", not good for those stood on the line.

The season was very successful, and we finished runners-up to Doubleday again. We had some high scores against the teams that finished at the bottom of the table, in particular Hertford United who we beat 10-1 and 9-3. We suffered two defeats, Doubleday beat us 0-3 and Keresdon Park 1-3. Overall we won 15 out of the 20 matches, drawing

3. We scored 84 goals and let in 33, suggesting that the defence needed tightening up.

In Cup matches, the first round tie against division 3 team Coombe Social, needed three games to get a result, Avondale eventually winning 2-1. We lost the next tie to Lanchester College 1-3.

At the start of the 1971-72 season, Grayson Minshaw resigned as secretary of the club. He hadn't had the opportunity to play many games during the season, and probably felt that it was time to hang his boots up. Barry Baker and Rod Prime also left. I took over as secretary, having done the job at Moseley United, and besides no one else wanted the job!

One of my first jobs was to raise enough cash to pay for a new set of shirts. Avondale played in the Newcastle strip, black and white striped shirts with red numbers on the back, black shorts and socks. This time there was a number 12 shirt to pay for, as the rules on the use of substitutes had been introduced, and of course, the goalkeepers jersey! I don't think for a minute that Team Managers realised that the use of substitutes could be tactical. We purchased the kit together with our lucky orange ball, from Nobby Mowe's Sport Supplies shop in Albany Road.

There was reorganisation in the League and reduced the number of divisions from five to four. Doubleday and Avondale were promoted to Division 2. The division had increased in size to fifteen teams. With cup matches, we would be playing, thirty two games minimum. Somebody must have predicted a mild winter!

The weather was good with no postponements for waterlogged pitches. We had a good season despite playing against stronger teams, and finished third, behind champions Doubleday, and runners-up Indian Commonwealth.

We won 18 of the 28 league matches, drew 4, and lost 6. Highest goals tally was 5, in wins against Exhall, Motor Panels, Indian New Star, and Meadway Rovers Reserves. We scored 72 goals and conceded 45. There were no easy games in this division, and we had to work hard to get a result.

In Coventry Evening Telegraph Junior Cup, we played teams from other leagues, beating Potters Green (Coventry Combination Division 1), by 2-1, and then losing to Wickman Reserves (Coventry Alliance Division 1), by 2-1.

In the President's Cup 1st round, we were drawn against Moseley United; I was made captain for the day, and was happy to win 2-1, after being 0-1 down. In the 2nd round, we played against another Division 1 team, Coachmakers, who we beat 2-1, and our luck ran out when we lost 2-1 to Whoberley Wanderers, also from Division 1.

At the start of the 1972/73 season, we were still in Division 2 and although we made an indifferent start to the season, Avondale would be Champions! Exhall finished runners-up with the same points total, but we had a better goal average. (Goal difference was not used then; goal average was a figure obtained by dividing the goals for by the goals against). Avondale had more or less repeated the form of last season, winning 17, drawing 5 and losing 4. We scored more goals (85) and conceded less (36).

In the cup competitions we lost 0-1 to Brandon & Wolston of the C&NW Senior Section, in the Coventry Evening Telegraph Junior Cup. In the Presidents Cup Meriden Rovers beat us 2-0. In the Boyd Carpenter Cup we beat two Coventry and District League teams, Hills Precision 3-0 and YCW 1-0, but lost out to Triumph Engineering Apprentices of the Coventry Alliance by 3-4 after extra time.

Looking back it was quite surprising that, for the three seasons I played for Avondale, they used less than twenty players. The captain and centre half Alan Hancox set the example to the team with no nonsense performances, ably supported by full back Rod Larcombe, who does everything at sixty miles per hour, including talking, and Tony Brown, our unsophisticated goalkeeper. I once wrote in the match report, that Tony had made a string of saves to win the game for us. It was published in "The Pink" the next week, Tony said "It wasn't that good, I thought I was rubbish". Credit, where credit is due!

The midfield engine room was John Bird, John Adams and Bob Colley all similar players, good in the tackle, good control, ability to beat an opponent with ease, and could read the game. What a motor John Bird had, he could beat man after man in surging runs. John Adams had height advantage and was strong in the air and on the ground, and scored goals. Tommy Small, an enigma! If you think of Tommy Hutchinson who played for CCFC, then Tommy Small is a similar type of player but quicker, and he scores more goals. A match winner! Bob Colley was a cultured player, he stroked the ball around. Ken Westgarth and Ray Staff vied for the right wing spot. Both players could beat their opponent, but lacked speed to breakaway. Good team men! Big Ron Osmond, the centre forward, was a good target man and would weigh in with his share of the goals.

    I played more of a defensive wing half, left back Barry Shipton wouldn't agree with that as he was always left with two men to mark! I didn't score many goals for Avondale, but the one I remember best was scored at Coundon Hall park, and the opponents goalie cleared the ball up field. I was positioned to head the ball, but without a challenge I decided to cushion head the ball. It didn't work to well and I remember one of my colleagues made some comment, but I managed to regain control of the ball, and set off on a strong run downfield. The midfield opened up and I went passed the last defenders, made an angle and slotted the ball home.

    There were several good goals scored, winger Tommy Small was quite a prolific scorer, and most were special, but probably the best goal was scored by Vic Saunders. We played YCW, a division 1 team, in the Leagues President's Cup, on pitch 1 at the Memorial park. We had lost the toss and had to kick down the slope in the first half, which was backs to the wall, and we survived an onslaught. In the second half, we got more into the game as YCW tended to overrun the ball down the slope, and they started arguing amongst themselves. Young Vic was of slight build and wasn't seeing much of the ball, but he had skill when given the time. Midway through the half, the ball arrived at his feet, with room around him and not under pressure, he teed the ball up and volleyed it from twenty five yards over the keepers head into the net. Goal of the Season!

There was no doubt in my mind that I made the right choice in leaving Moseley United to come and play for Avondale FC. The atmosphere in the dressing room was different. On the pitch everyone played for each other, and there was no moaning if you made a mistake, only encouragement. The other thing that comes to mind is – tactics! In matches that we lost or drew, we talked about the opposing players who gave us the most problems. The next time we played them, we made sure that those players were given special attention, and it worked.

In particular, the two games against Rayon Rangers, played on pitches 1 and 2 at the Memorial park. We drew the first game 3-3, and won the second game 4-1. We realised that two players, the left winger and the inside right were dictating the game, and their left back was not happy if put under pressure. It was a pity that we didn't realise this during the first game, but the tactics were quite simple for the second game. Do not give these players room, crowd them, harry them, hurt them. The inside right went missing for most of the match, one hard but fair tackle did the job (no, it wasn't me). The left back was forced into mistake after mistake, and the service to the left winger was curtailed. It wasn't a totally different game to the first one, but we were in control from start to finish.

The team had a chance to show how good it was, when we played Triumph Engineering Apprentices in a Telegraph Cup match at Fletchamstead Highway. In winter the games used to kick off early to ensure that there was enough daylight to see the ball. The weather was dull and overcast and the light was not good when we kicked off. The Triumph team was in the Coventry Alliance League, and in the opening minutes it was obvious that we had a game on our hand. Young Vic Saunders was playing at centre forward, and he was keen to shine, as his brother was playing for the opposition! Avondale worked hard and were a match for the hosts, the tie ending in a 3-3 draw at full time. Extra time was played and near the end of the second period, Triumph broke away to score the winning goal in the gloom. Yes, Vic's brother scored! Despite the loss I really enjoyed the game, and that's what it is all about.

I had been playing for Barras Green WMC on Sundays and their manager was keen for me to play on Saturdays as well. I regarded some of the Avondale team as brothers, we had a good bond, and it was a difficult decision to leave them, but I didn't have time for regrets.

Avondale, were still going strong in 1979/80 season in Division 1, having been relegated and promoted in the intervening years. They also reached the final of the Leagues' President's Cup.

Barras WMC - Founded 1966
Barras Green Rangers – Founded 1970

Barras Green Working Man's Club ran two football teams. When I first started playing for them in season 1972/73, Barras Green Rangers played in the Coventry and District Sunday League, and Barras WMC played in the Coventry and Central Warwickshire League, also on a Sunday.

At home we were expecting our first baby, and Eileen wanted me to be at home more. I had finished playing Sunday football with Parkstone WMC, but was playing for Avondale on Saturday.

Before I got married, I had been a member of the Parkstone WMC which was just down the road from where I lived. After I married Eileen, we lived in Courthouse Green, and I became a member of the Barras WMC club soon after. Eileen's Dad and Jimmy, her brother, were members there. John Pinnegar, the Barras manager, had wanted me to play for his teams for some time, and I had played a game for one of the teams at the end of the last season, to prove my ability as such.

The Barras teams played on the pitches behind "the Bolshey" the Barras Public House, and alongside Stoke Heath School. The pitches were on the small side, but well grassed compared to those on Stoke Heath common opposite.

The teams had a variety of strips, but usually all white or all red. We once had to play in a recently acquired full set of kit, sky blue shirts with collars and black shorts and socks. Nobody had checked the strip before it was handed out. The atmosphere was as blue as the shirts; the kit was made to fit a school team! Somehow we managed to squeeze into it, and play the match; really funny!

The season started and I was playing for the Rangers team in the Coventry and District (Sunday) League - Senior Division 5. The first match was against Coventry AEC on the day that my daughter Wendy was born. We won 3-0 and I scored from the penalty spot. This was followed by a 9-0 victory over Stoneleigh and 10-1 against Sovereign, both teams would end up at the bottom of the division.

It was becoming clear that Barras wasn't the only high scoring team in the Division, as Daytona Sports, Nighthawks and Devon Wanderers were also making the net bulge frequently. The Local Soccer Round-up in the Pink for this season was lacking in the results for Barras matches against the leading clubs, but we beat Devon Wanderers 2-1, and lost to Nighthawks 3-5 and Daytona Sports 0-3. We also lost twice to A.C. X1 by the odd goal! In a four week period we completed the double over Unbrako 10-0 and 4-2, and White Bear 7-2 and 8-3. Overall, we finished 5th in the Division behind champions Daytona Sports, winning 13, drawing 2, and losing 7. We scored 92 goals and let in 42.

The cup trail pitched us against teams that were in Division 4. In the Transport Shield we lost 1-2 to Mason Utd, and in the Challenge Cup we beat Coventry Transport 4-3 and Strollers 7-2. The 3rd round tie was played before Christmas and the opponents and score are not known, but we didn't make it into the fourth round!

Barras WMC were having an up and down season finishing 7th of 10 teams, winning 6, drawing 1 and losing 11, scoring 38 goals and conceding 68. Padmore Rovers won the title, with Coronation Club Reserves runners-up.

The start of the 1973/74 season began with the team squads interchanged. I don't know which bright spark thought of this, but it was the start of a remarkably successful period for the club which would bring cup and league titles. Unfortunately, one team would struggle to get results.

So, after playing for the Rangers in the Coventry and District Sunday League, the squad, myself included, now Barras WMC, were in Division 2 of the Coventry and Central Warwickshire (Sunday) League. The team was stronger than last season and some of the opposition not so good. It was a good start to the season, winning nine games before drawing the next two. Points were dropped against close rivals Standard Bearer, Midland Bank and then Courthouse. Indeed, it was Courthouse who inflicted the only defeat 2-3.

Barras WMC had to win one of its last two games to win the Division 2 title, we won both. As usual at the end of a season some matches have to be played in the evening, due to postponements earlier in the season. The final match of the season was against Corinthians. The touchline was packed with supporters and members from the club.

The game kicked off, and within five minutes Corinthians had scored. It took us about ten minutes to equalise and then we couldn't stop scoring. Each goal was met with a roar of approval, and we ran out 19-1 winners. Bobby Halcrow scored 7, Dave Buckingham 5 and Jack Foley 4. Two of Bobby's goals were volleys hit from the corner of the penalty area, great skill and power! Everything came together that night, and nearly every attempt on goal was on target, and most goals were unstoppable. Corinthians changed their goalkeeper, but the replacement couldn't stem the flood of goals, but they battled to the final whistle.

Barras WMC still had another game to play. We had battled through the rounds of the Tom Cooke Cup. The final was played at the Butts Stadium against Newtown Athletic. The match is reported elsewhere in the book, but the Pink wrote that it was splendid entertainment, and we won 4-3. A Cup and League double – Brilliant!

The Coventry and District Sunday Football League had reorganised the divisional set up, and it meant that Barras Green Rangers were to battle against most of the teams that they had faced last season, including Daytona Sports, Nighthawks, and Devon Wanderers, in what was now Division 4.

Nighthawks won the league scoring 133 goals in 22 matches, and Daytona Sports scored 99 goals to finish second. Barras Green Rangers sadly finished bottom of the division. They managed to win 4 matches and draw 2, but had two points deducted, probably for playing an unregistered player.

For the 1974/75 season, the psychic who had masterminded the interchange of team personnel last season, decided to withdraw Barras Green Rangers from Sunday Football, and apply for membership of the Coventry and District (Saturday) Football League. The application was accepted and the team placed in Section 'B'. Barras WMC would continue in the Coventry and Central Warwickshire (Sunday) League, but now in Division 1.

Manager John Pinnegar decided both teams should be of equal strength. To do that you need the same eleven players to play Saturday and Sunday, but not all players wanted to do this. I am sure that John didn't want a repeat of last season's situation, whereby one team collected the trophies and the other team got the wooden spoon! Whatever he decided it worked! He managed to get a squad together that could produce the goods. Some players would be unhappy because they couldn't get a game at the weekend. They had two choices, stick with it –they could get a game if someone left or got injured, alternatively, there were plenty of other clubs who needed players!

These Barras teams were a good blend of youth and experience. Some of the young lads had just left school, and the others were not old enough to drink in the Social Club after the game.

Not all players turned out Saturday and Sunday, but the team selection hardly made a difference to the team performance. The goalkeepers John Phelan and Dick Senior were both gutsy, and never pulled out of a challenge. John was one of the best goalkeepers I had played alongside, not necessarily in performance, but in the way he marshalled the defence and organised them at corners and freekicks. Dick couldn't kick a dead ball to save his life, so I took the goalkicks!

Alan Brick was the commanding centre half, backed up by Pete Glynn, and me at full backs. The creative midfield was chosen from

Micky John, Alan Hill, Billy Masters and Eddie Rooney. The team was fortunate to have some good young players in Grant Farquharson, Kevin and Dud Foley, Colin Rust, Pete Johnson and Kevin Mulhearn. They were all good on the ball, and provided the service to goalscorers Bobby Halcrow, Jack Foley and Dave Buckingham. Squad players such as Pete Timms, Martin Glynn, Danny O'Connor and John Neil were always available to play.

The team and manager were ably supported at most games by Brian Clough, Bob Thompson, Jimmy Peterson (my brother-in-law), Billy Glynn and Dave McOwat.

Barras Green Rangers (the Saturday team), got off to a high scoring start with 10-0 win against Bubbenhall Reserves, 8-1 against SNR, and 11-1 against New Hillfields. The team was brought down to earth, losing the next game to Edgewick 1-2. The opposition in the division wasn't the best and most teams suffered heavy defeats. To their credit Bubbenhall Reserves put up a strong resistance in the return fixture losing by the odd goal in three.

At the end of February most teams had played all their fixtures, and the league started a Supplementary Cup competition, whereby the top five and the bottom five played in mini-divisions, and the winners of both divisions played for a trophy.

This was bad news for both our Saturday and Sunday teams, we were victims of our own success in the league and cup competitions. Then it rained and rained! Postponements meant that we would be playing four games a week. This took a toll and injuries weakened the team. The results suffered inasmuch that we lost another game to Cheylesmore 0-2 and drew two other games against teams that we had hammered earlier in the season. Edgewick won the title, dropping only three points, we had beaten them in the return fixture 5-1. We were runners-up scoring 107 goals and conceding just 23.

In the Supplementary Cup we topped our division and we beat New Hillfields 3-0 in the play off. In other cup matches, we lost to Alliance team Kingfield 1-3. In the Invitation Cup, the first round tie against Keresdon Park was marred by a crude tackle on Dave Buckingham, which broke his leg. We made sure that we won the tie after Dave had gone to Hospital. The second round went to a replay against GNP Reserves, which we lost 1-2.

In the Coventry Evening Telegraph Minor Cup, we made steady progress through the rounds beating District Section 'A' team Hertford 6-2, Surburban IV team Phoenix, and District Division 3 team Tile Hill OB Reserves 2-1. The semi-final against Minster Rangers was described by the Referee John Jackson "This was a superb example of how football should be played. Both teams were a credit to the competition and it was unfortunate that one side had to lose". The game was stale mate at full time both teams scoring twice, but Barras went on to win 4-3, although fortunate to win on the day!

The final is described elsewhere in the book, but after a long and sometimes difficult season, Barras Green Rangers got the reward for their efforts, beating Surburban IV league team Clifton 2-1 after extra time. Brilliant!!!

Whilst all that was happening, Barras WMC were having their own battles on Sunday mornings. The headlines in 'The Pink' on Saturday April 5, 1975 told the story of the team's success so far this season. "At last 'Green' lose a game". Yes, we had lost a league match to Minster Rangers 1-3. The report continued, "After a run of 16 successive wins which had taken them to the quarter finals of the VL Edmonds Cup, the Final of the FH Ogg cup and second place in Senior Division 1, Barras, with one game in hand, now trail leaders Celtic Travellers by three points, but have a superior goal average. These two sides have yet to meet in the league, so the destiny of this championship will be undecided for some time"

Well it took just two weeks; we completed the double over the Travellers, beating them 3-0 in both matches to take the league title. We also took the FH Ogg cup, beating Bridge End Reserves 2-1, the decider was an own goal by the Bridge End keeper.

The VL Edmonds Cup first round tie was against Premier Division 2 team Padmore Rovers. The tie was described as an excellent attacking game, which ended in a 5-4 victory for Barras, the winning goal was an own goal! The second round matched us with Celtic Travellers and we despatched them 7-2.

The third round was against another Premier 2 team, Sovereign. Jack Foley and Bobby Halcrow scored two goals each in the 4-1 victory. Our luck ran out in the quarter-final against Premier 1 side Glade, defensive errors led to a 1-4 defeat.

I had missed some games this season, with a gashed ankle, courtesy of a Bridge End player, and a pulled thigh muscle, which wasn't as painful as the ankle, but I couldn't run or kick a ball for weeks, luckily I didn't miss too many games due to the bad weather, but John Pinnegar came and dragged me out the house when he was faced with the fixture back log. I wasn't the only player missing due to injury or work commitments, and it was the squad players, who had stood on the touchline for most of the season, that grabbed their opportunity and played their hearts out for the club.

There is no doubt that the goals scored by Bobby Halcrow, Jack Foley and Dave Buckingham, was paramount in the success over the last three seasons.

I scored a few goals for the Barras teams, but you don't get many chances playing full back, most of them from the penalty spot, until Billy Masters took over, the occasional fluke from a corner kick or an over hit cross, and annoyingly, a couple of own goals!

One of my better goals was similar to one that I scored for Avondale, inasmuch that I collected the ball in our half and went forward, the midfield opened up, and let me through, the opposing centre half came to tackle me but was too slow and I ghosted past him and slotted the ball into the near corner of the goal. I think this was the game that we won 10-0 and Jack Foley scored eight goals. He had the ball on a stick that day. He ran and ran, beating opponents with ease, as if their feet were stuck in the mud. What an achievement! What energy!

Before the 1975/76 Season, Eileen reminded me that I had promised to spend more time at home, by not playing football on Saturday or Sundays, or both. I wanted to play for the Barras Club on both days and it would be difficult deciding which day not to!

At the start of the season the team lost some players, Colin Rust, Pete Johnson, Bobby Halcrow and Billy Masters, which left a big hole in midfield. I was keen to move up front having played full back for three seasons; there were squad players good enough to fill in at full back. I was disappointed when it didn't happen and I then considered finding another team.

After last season's successes, both the Saturday and Sunday teams had been promoted. Barras Green Rangers were now in Section 'A' of the Coventry and District (Saturday) Football League, and Barras WMC in the Coventry and Central Warwickshire Premier League Division 2.

The youngsters in the team had matured and were playing well together, the football flowed better and there was less long ball, and more passing. It was always good to win a match, even better to hammer the opposition, but the first games were more enjoyable! Don't get me wrong, I used the long ball perhaps more than anybody, and it had served Barras well for years. The other noticeable change was that the young lads didn't hold onto the ball, it was 'push and run', whereas before some players had to beat an opponent, and then another, sometimes getting bogged down in midfield, and losing possession.

After a few weeks Eddie Rooney was signed to boost the midfield, and Bobby Halcrow returned, the grass not being greener in the other field! The kids lost their team place and it was back to the long ball. No disrespect to either player but the next few games were not so enjoyable. Billy Masters also returned later in the year.

I spoke to my best mate John, I hadn't seen him for a while; family's sometime get in the way of friendships. He was playing for Apollo Rangers on Sundays; he worked with some of the team members at Morris Engines. He suggested that I turned up and watched them, bring my kit in case they're one short.

It was difficult to explain my reasons for leaving to Barras manager John Pinnegar, it would have been easy to make excuses and lay blame etc, but I just wanted a change of scene and wanted to play only on a Sunday. I've made snap decisions before and fortunately none have come back to bite me. I was fortunate to play for the Barras, and we had some good times, but it was time for me to move on. Barras would be just as successful without me; it was in the stars! The season progressed and the prophecy was fulfilled.

The Saturday team won Section 'A' dropping only one point from the 22 matches, they scored 106 goals and conceded only 21. The team reached the semi-final of the League's Invitation Cup, before losing to Cheylesmore Social by the odd goal in three.

The Boyd-Carpenter Cup semi-final tie against Division 1 side Foleshill Athletic was the "Star Junior Match" in 'The Pink'. The report describes the match as a game of two halves, with Foleshill taking the initiative, restricting Barras to breakaways. Foleshill were well on top and led 3-0 at half time, despite losing a player with an injury requiring hospital treatment. Barras came into the game more in the second half, but couldn't turn the pressure into goals, with poor finishing and a confident display by the Foleshill goalkeeper.

The Sunday team won the Premier Division 2 title winning 15 games, drawing 1 and losing 2, scoring 84 goals and conceding 33. The team reached the final of the Tom Owen Cup at the Butts Stadium. The game went to extra-time and Dave Buckingham scored the vital goal to give Barras a 2-1 victory over Celtic Travellers.

Well done men, I knew you wouldn't let me down!

The Barras Green WMC club was still running two teams at the end of the 1970's, and were always there or thereabouts in challenging for league and cup honours.

Apollo Rangers (Colliers FC)

Apollo Rangers FC was formed by a group of employees at the Morris Engines plant in Courthouse Green in 1971, and played in Division 6 of the Coventry and District Sunday League. In their first season, they had only played a handful of games, when they made headline news in 'The Pink', "Apollo Power Puts Out Holders". Indeed, they had taken on and beaten Division 1 team Park Rangers, who were last season's winners of the Coventry and District Leagues' Transport Shield. This was no fluke, Apollo won 5-1 convincingly.

It was part way through the 1975/76 season and I had finished with Barras Green WMC. John Colledge suggested that I turn up for the next Apollo game. He had told the club committee that I was the man to solve Apollo's goal scoring problem. He forgot to tell the manager that I'd been playing full back for the last three or four years.

The club, now in Divison 4, played their home matches at Sowe Common. The pitches were flat and drained well, however, the pitch usually allocated to Apollo was next to the canal, and although there were plenty of trees, the ball had to be rescued from the canal on many occasions! The local pub, The Jolly Colliers, was the meeting point for an after match drink, and the landlord would cross over the M6 motorway footbridge to watch us play, for a short time before opening up! It was also good to see that some of the original founder members of the club turned up to watch the team play. The team played in white shirts and sky blue shorts and socks, and had an all red second kit.

It was early November, and I had not played since leaving Barras Green WMC. It is always difficult to fit into a new team part way through the season. Some of the positions in the team were settled, but with the rest it was a case of mix and match, and Apollo had a centre forward playing in goal!

The first games told me that this team was not on the same level as Barras Green WMC, and it needed some stability and a few stronger players! I enjoyed playing up front with the freedom to roam. I found that my years of playing in the defence gave me an advantage, inasmuch that I could anticipate what the opposing defender next move would be.

The match results were variable, but I was pleased with the way I had fitted into the team. In most games I had chances to score, but hit the bar, or dragged a shot wide, or the goalkeeper had saved. My first goal was a penalty, although the keeper did get a hand to the ball, and I managed to score four more before the end of the season. I had taken the responsibility for corner kicks and was to score some goals direct from corners. Taking the kick from the right wing with my left foot I could swing the ball high into the goal. The other players in the team knew what was coming and pressured the defence and the goalkeeper. Some keepers just weren't brave enough.

The following season 1976/77, the team looked more settled and the Team Manager, Malc Wrighton, played a 4-3-3 system, which suited the players he had available; unfortunately, it meant that some of the stalwarts of the club couldn't always get a game. We had a new goalkeeper, a young lad Paul (Chalky) White, who worked in the local butchers, which was helpful around Christmas time! The back four could be selected from Gerald Perry, Kevin Mullen, Sid Hussey, John MacHendry (Mr Versatile), Kevin Harridence and Brian Dixon. The midfield four selected from John Colledge, Colin Daniels, Gaz Tyrell, John Garner and Bobby Caves. The front three was selected from Ken Whitehead, Lol Anderson, Reg Shepherd, Alan Goodman and myself. Other squad players were Trevor Hill, Keith Brearley and Paul Whitehead. The team performance was stronger and more solid with a natural goalkeeper between the posts, (no disrespect to Reg Shepherd, who had volunteered last season).

The results were good from the start, and I was enjoying my football and scoring goals. I ended the season with twenty eight, a club record, so I was told. In two of the matches I scored four goals, the first match was against Mowog (another team formed by Morris Engines workers), which Apollo won 5-2, and the second match against Herbert Athletic, Apollo winning 5-1.

The match against Mowog was played on Sowe Common with a very strong wind blowing across the pitch. It was a competitive game despite the conditions, and during the first half, I collected the ball just inside the opponents half on the right wing, and tried to put the ball through to the centre forward. I had to use my weaker right foot and over hit the ball. It went high and long and the wind caught it, and despite the best efforts of the Mowog goalkeeper it flew into the far corner of the goal. What a fluke! My second goal of the game was from a corner in the second half. I found space in the box and headed the excellent cross into the net at the angle of post and crossbar. There is a sense of achievement, and special about scoring a goal with your head. Probably because it was the only headed goal I scored! It's strange, but I can't recall the other two goals, possibly some slight concussion from the header.

The match against Herberts was played on their ground in Crabmill Lane. The first goal was a burst into the penalty area; the ball came to me from a poor clearance and I saw gap and toed the ball over two defenders and ran between them, as the ball came down I was fortunate to block the ball against an opponent's leg and it ran clear for me to smash it high into the net from a few yards. The second was a scramble in their goalmouth, and the third goal resulted from a long clearance from our defence, the Herbert's centre half dithered, and I robbed him of the ball and pushed it passed the advancing goalkeeper. The fourth, and probably the best, was again from a long high clearance out of our defence, which the centre half misjudged and it bounced over him, I took it on the next bounce and volleyed it over the keeper into the roof of the net.

There were other memorable goals like the two I scored against City Treasurers at the Municipal Sports Ground (Now the Alan Higgs Sports Trust). Apollo had managed to get the services of Ken Whitehead, who I understand, played Southern League football at that time. He was a class player, and gave the team a lift. He played centre forward and scored fourteen goals in as many matches.

The match was going to be tough as the opponents were in the top two in the league. During the first half playing down the slope we had competed well, but were 1-0 down. The play was in the middle of the opponents half, and the ball came to Ken, and he laid it in my path, I didn't need to change stride and hit it with my right foot (again) and it screamed toward the goal. The Treasurer's goalkeeper was caught on the hop, but made ground across his goal and dived; he managed to get his fingers to the ball, but couldn't stop it hitting the net.

The second goal, which proved to be the winner, was in the second half. Kicking up the slope, we came more into the game and I chased an over-hit pass to put pressure on the full back and keeper. The keeper had come out of his goal along the goal line near to the edge of the penalty area. I went to the full back, who instead of leathering the ball downfield, tried to make a back pass to the keeper, but under hit it. I got to the ball just before the keeper could pick it up, and tackled him, the ball broke loose and I walked it into the net.

We had a good match against the Coventry Evening Telegraph team at their Lythalls Lane ground, Holbrooks. They were captained by Ken Widdows, the Sport Editor at that time. We won 6-3 in an evenly balanced match. I had possession and the opponents were encamped on the penalty area. I went from left to right intending to take a shot; I got a shout from half back John Garner and as I ran past him I stepped on the ball. Apparently, all the defenders were following me and were caught wrong footed when John took his shot, unfortunately, it was straight at the keeper! It's the unexpected that beats defences!

There was a cup match against Parkstone WMC first team at Longford Park. It was a few years since I had played for them, but there were familiar faces, including my brother Roger. Apollo were playing well, and I was out to impress. I didn't get the chance, Parkstone easily ran out 4-0 winners.

A disallowed goal can be more frustrating than hitting the cross-bar from thirty yards. Occasionally manager Malc would play me on the right, instead of my natural left. I had to adapt but I could cross with my right foot, but never seemed to get the same power and accuracy. In one game I was attacking down the right and went inside to beat the opposing full back, he caught my right leg and I stumbled, but managed to keep on my feet and took a shot with my left foot and the ball flew into the net off the far post. The referee had blown as I took my shot, and disallowed the goal and awarded the free kick. I wasn't happy about him not playing the advantage, but he was of the opinion that I was going to fall after the tackle. He wouldn't change his mind.

My first full season with Apollo Rangers had started well and ended well, we won the last six league games, but there was a slump in mid season that put paid to any medal hopes. The biggest win was 12-0 against Pegasus with Lol Anderson scoring four and Bobby Caves three. Apollo finished fourth, winning 13 out of 22 matches.

The next season 1977/78 was a similar, which was a bit of a surprise, because Apollo Rangers were now in Division 3. Although we were playing against teams that we knew, the games would be tougher.

I was scoring goals again, but not as often as last season. I put it down to service. With Lol Anderson playing central striker and more of the ball coming down the middle, I lacked service. Lol was a good goalscorer on his day but sometimes held the ball too long, and yet he could be an excellent provider and made space for other players. In midfield John Garner and Colin Daniels pushed forward more for goals. The team's performance was more solid and results were better.

The other factor was Sowe Common. The Parks Department had opened up four new pitches that ran east-west rather than north-south, not that it made any difference, but the pitches were bigger than the existing ones that we had been playing on. I found the pitches tiring and the turf cloying, which was strange because the field drained well. I was running further and seeing less of the ball.

In one of our first games on one of the new pitches, we had gone 4-0 up in about fifteen minutes, by coincidence Lol had collected a ball down the right and sent over a glorious cross, which I netted without breaking stride. As the game progressed defences took control, and the service to Apollo's front men broke down through over hit or under hit passing, or late passing resulting in offsides, or just not releasing the ball. If I went looking for the ball, it would be passed to the vacant space. It was a pattern that was to occur frequently.

We had some good results winning four games on the bounce, then undo all the good work by losing the next two. Perhaps the best result was against eventual league winners Eastern Green, played at Meriden. It was a tough game and the opposition were on top, playing down the slope, but we dug in and in the second half I scored two, one direct from a corner and the other from thirty yards, the ball went through the goalkeeper hands and passed just under the bar. Eastern Green got their revenge in the return, winning 1-6, at the end of the season. Apollo finished fourth in the league, with similar results to the previous season.

The club took on a new name in the summer. Apollo Rangers became Colliers FC. The team also had a sponsor in Nuneaton Engineering, ending the worry about the cost of replacement kit! There had been a long association with the Jolly Collier public house probably because it was the nearest pub to Sowe Common, where the team played their home matches. The manager and his wife were supportive of the team, and would occasionally provide some food after games.

This season with Colliers was to be my last. Eileen was expecting our second child, and I had agreed to stop playing at the end of the season.

There were some new faces in the team, and half the team now played together for Jet Blades on a Saturday! In November, after we had won six and lost three games, then we played Unbrako. We outplayed the opposition and rattled in five goals, including one of my inswinging corners, when they broke away and scored, without any of our defence making a tackle. I was a bit disgusted, as it went against my competitive nature. I walked off the pitch in disgust, much to everyone's amazement!

There was a meeting during the week, and I had chance to explain my actions and apologise, I was told that I would be suspended for the next two games. This hit home later, when I learned that the second fixture was against Barras Green WMC at Stoke Heath. They had quit the Coventry and Central Warwickshire League, and been given a place in our Division.

The day of the match arrived and I turned up with my boots, and as it turned out Apollo only had the bare eleven. The team manager, Malc Wrighton asked me to get changed, and I went to the pitch as substitute. The Barras team were a bit surprised that I wasn't playing, until I told them what I had done. The Barras youngsters won the day 4-2, Kevin Mulhearn scoring two. We had an injury to one of the players late on, but Malc would rather play with ten men, than play me. The manager had made his point. It proved to be the beginning of the end for me at The Colliers.

1979 was a bad year for snow and ice, and we would struggle to get a game in January and February. The first game back after the enforced break was against Alvis Sports and Social. The fixture was supposed to be at Sowe Common, but the ground was still frozen. Alvis suggested transferring the game to their ground at Holyhead Road. Unfortunately the frost returned on Saturday night, and when we turned up the sun had melted the frost and the top surface was remarkably soft but underneath it was rutted and bone hard. We delayed the start for a while and the groundsman spread a bit of sand. The game shouldn't have been played but we all wanted to play! I found it really hard going and didn't adapt to the pitch. Some areas were ok and others like a skating rink, but we gritted our teeth and lost 1-5.

For days after the game, I was in agony. I had suffered pains and inflammation in my hands and feet for weeks now, and was taking anti-inflammatory tablets. Some aches and pains were to be expected after the match, as it was like pre-season training all over again! This was different, the pain and stiffness was also in my shoulders and neck, which made me nauseus. On top of this I wasn't happy at work, and the situation there was getting me stressed, and Eileen was weeks away from producing our second child. Time to hang up my boots! The end of an illustrious career, it had been fun!

Part 3   Football Matters

Sunday Football

Before I tell you about the start of Sunday football in Coventry, it's worth illustrating what Sundays were like in the 1950's. The aftermath of World War II haunted the end of the 1940's; the inevitable rationing due to lack of basic foods, and the problems of finding work for thousands of people and rebuilding the Britain's services.

Life in the 1950's was improving all the time, but life was simple then, Foleshill was a village, there was everything that you needed to live comfortably. You had your bread and milk delivered to the doorstep by men driving a horse and cart, and the Coal man would deliver a hundredweight of coal or nutty slack, but he wouldn't put it under the stairs in the bogey hole for you!

On the Foleshill Road, there was a Chemist shop, a Butcher shop, a Television and Radio shop, a Fruit and Vegetable shop, Newsagents, Ladies and a Gentleman's Hairdressers, a Dress shop and two Pubs, The William and The Wheatsheaf.

Toward Longford, at New Inn Bridge there was also a General Store, Post Office and an Off License. The Dovedale Cinema was just over the canal bridge. In the other direction toward the City centre, along Foleshill Road in the area called the Depot (the Coventry Tram Depot was there), there was a Decorating Shop, Electrical Shop, Post Office, Chemist, Doctor's Surgery, Barbers, and an Opticians named Hugh Seymour (get it!). Further on, is Great Heath and the shopping centre, known as the 'General Wolfe', taken from the local pub. There was the Regal Cinema, Banks, Maypole, Bicycle shop, and Co-op stores, one of which was a large muti-storey Emporium that sold clothes, beds and furniture, televisions, and washing machines. In Livingstone Road was the Swimming Baths. In Lythalls Lane there was a Fish and Chip shop, a Pet Shop that also sold Fishing Tackle, and another pub The Olde Hall (my regular, but not in the fifties), and in the other direction, another General Store and a Wood Yard. If you need more you, could go to the Corner Shop in Elmsdale Road, which sold bread and milk and cooked meats, and a variety of tinned products to feed the hungry family.

The redevelopment of the Coventry City centre after the bombing in the war, attracted all the major stores; Owen Owen, Marks and Spencer, British Home Stores and Woolworths all had large shops in the new Precincts, and these shops offered the buyers - choice!

So, you can see that life was simple, everything was laid on a plate, and within easy grasp. The problem was that on Sunday everything shut down; everything that is except for the Newsagents and the Pubs. The papers had to be delivered, so the shops would open until twelve at the latest, the same time that the Pubs would be opening. They were allowed to open for two hours and then re-open at seven until half ten.

The children of the fifties and sixties will probably only remember their mother's Sunday dinners, mainly because there was a pudding afterwards! Apart from that, the only thing that happened, was that they had to go to Church, Chapel or Sunday School. Generally, Mum was exhausted from preparing and eating the dinner, Dad was asleep after four or more pints at the pub and not eating his dinner, and the bored kids weren't allowed out!

The Sunday Trading Act 1950 had a lot to answer for. The bill was to cause confusion; it allowed shops to open, but restricted the sale of most goods! When you went into a shop, you would be confronted by swathes of brown paper covering most of the display. This wasn't to stop the chocolate turning white, or to keep the flies and wasps off – it was to stop you buying certain products.

Eventually most shops gave up and closed. The bigger stores were against Sunday opening on religious ground, and also worried about the additional cost of paying staff. The act would be repealed partly in 1986 and fully in 1994, when restriction on trading hours was the only limitation.

All of this doesn't affect football, there was no restriction on the freedom to play any sport, although the religious amongst us would insist that 'Sunday was a day of rest'.

The 'victory babies' had grown into strapping teenagers and had lots of energy to use up. People's attitudes were changing, and they were asking question of the establishment, hence the CND/Ban the Bomb rally in London in 1960, which attracted 100,000 protestors.

The Football Association allowed Sunday football, but it was only popular in the London, Stafford, and Northern Areas. There became a demand for Sunday football in Coventry and surrounding towns. Jimmy Hill had been made manager at Coventry City FC and had launched the Sky Blue Revolution. Amateur footballers in the city were now keen to support their hometown team after years of disappointment, but still wanted to play the game also. Sunday football was the answer. It would also be invaluable for shift workers, and shop workers, who were contracted to work on a Saturday

It needed someone to get the ball rolling and the push came from Garlicks Ltd, a local Building Contractor, and one of their employees Ken Prestwich. 'The Pink' (Saturday January 12, 1963) reported that a meeting had been held that week at the Telegraph's offices, at which the Coventry and District Sunday Football League was officially formed, and a Committee elected. Mr Prestwich said that there was great potential in Coventry for Sunday football, and that a minimum of eight teams were required to form a league.

The eight would then register with Birmingham County Football Association, and when the registrations are received by the league, it would apply for affiliation to the BCFA. Mr Prestwich thought that there was little doubt that the Parks Department would keep some pitches open on a Sunday.

Representatives from local leagues attended the meeting alongside representatives of teams that already play on Sundays, albeit friendly matches. Garlicks Ltd are unable to field a team on a Saturday, but could possibly field two teams on the Sunday. To cement their commitment to the new league, Mr H R Garlick, the President of the new formed league, donated a Cup and presented it to the Chairman of the newly formed league Mr M Malone. It would be known as that President's Cup.

Things were moving fast and two weeks later Mr Prestwich informed 'The Pink' that ten teams had registered with the BCFA and the league had now applied for affiliation. Other clubs had expressed an interest and a closing date for clubs to join this season was fixed at February 6, 1963. The provisional date for the kick off was set for February 17.

The new league had raised the hackles of a number of Saturday leagues that use parks pitches to play on. They were complaining about the suggestion that some parks pitches would be kept free for Sunday football.

Mr A G Haughton, secretary of the Coventry Combination, whose teams play on a Saturday. He said that the Parks Department agree that there are not enough pitches to go round and he dreads to think what state the playing surfaces will deteriorate into after a spell of bad weather.

Mr Haughton also raised the issue of players who turn out for different clubs on a Saturday and Sunday may be Cup-tied. He continued that he thought there was sufficient leagues in the area, and highlighted the problem of teams failing to raise a full side, or cancelling the fixture or at worse resigning halfway through the season.

He suggested that a drastic pruning of these inefficient clubs would enable the remaining ones to become stronger, and with fewer teams there would be more referees to cover matches. What planet was he on!

The first fixtures for the Coventry and District Sunday League on February 17, 1963, list below, show two divisions of eight teams. The competition would be run on a league basis, and the two top teams in both sections will meet to compete for the Presidents Cup.

Section A
Wood End v Post Office Sports
Avondale v Coventry Evening Telegraph
Wolston Dynamos v Coventry Auctioneers
Devon Wanderers v Morris Motors

Section B
Ryton v HA Smiths
Caledonians v St James
Garlicks v Coventry Indian Workers
Webster and Bennet v Foleshill Co-op

The Sunday League was up and running. A lot of work went on behind the scenes, and Chairman David Schofield and Ken Prestwich approached Vic Terry and his wife Beryl, to establish a workable administration system, and sort the fixtures for all the matches and make the necessary arrangements for pitches and referees. Vic persuaded fellow referee Frank Lyddieth to help and between the three of them, working long into the night managed to get a viable system.

During the sixties there was an emergence of Indian teams. The first team was the Indian Workers. Initially, the teams were weak and let in a bucketful of goals. Young Indian lads took the game seriously, and you could see groups of them playing football, during the summer months on parks around Coventry. I worked alongside the first Indian apprentice at Wickman. Kebbi told me that they could only play football until they got married, then they would not be allowed. He said they concentrated on one and two touch football, and played without goals, just trying to keep the ball from the other team.

Avondale played against his team, and we struggled to contain them. I felt that they hadn't learned the art of tackling, and at times this led to confrontation. Additionally, feelings were running high in Coventry, areas of the city couldn't cope with the influx of immigrants, and there were thousands more on the way. Racism was rife.

One of the Barras Green WMC games, was against an Indian team, at Stoke Heath. The game sparked interest locally as the Barras Working Men's Club was about to taken over by Indians. There was a good crowd lining the pitch and the match was about to start. In hindsight the Referee wasn't up to the job, and lost control of the game at times. It was a difficult game to referee as there was a lot of off-the-ball incidents, as well as tackles flying in from both sides. The players of both sides were annoyed at decisions, or lack of them; and the crowd were also baying for blood! I'll give the referee some credit for sticking at it, and things quietened down after a few names were scribbled in his book. The result was not important.

As the number of Indian teams increased, the novelty wore off and they were accepted, just as was the fact that Coventry was becoming multi-cultural.

The touch paper on the rocket that was the Coventry and District Sunday Football League had been lit and there was no stopping lift-off! Ten years later, The Pink published an article (14.04.1973), recording the achievements of the league in the first ten years.

"Dream comes true for District". A Gimmick....It will not last....no-one will take it seriously – these were some of the criticisms put forward when Sunday football was launched 10 years ago.

Sabbath soccer has not only confounded the critics, it has proved to be a bigger success than even the diehard pioneers dared hope!
Just nine clubs originally expressed an interest when the Coventry and District Sunday Football Leagues were formed back in 1963. . . . now membership is past the 140 mark and other leagues continue to thrive in the city.

The history of the District Leagues was recalled at the tenth anniversary dinner at the Hotel Leofric, and it was fitting on this occasion – in front of a distinguished gathering of representatives of the game at national and local level – that the go-ahead was announced for the bold development scheme at Tile Hill.

The Leagues have been planning for several years to establish their own headquarters and playing facilities, and their dreams should come to reality within the next 12-18 months. This is all possible because of the remarkable success of their development fund launched some three years ago. In addition to boosting the funds of clubs and providing all players with insurance cover, the fund has given the Leagues a bigger financial shot in the arm than anyone expected.

Without giving away too many secrets, it can be said that the Leagues are now making a profit in excess of four figures a year – all of which will be put back into the game via the much awaited Tile Hill development.

Yes, the standing of the District leagues in Coventry soccer circles is far detached from those ill-informed comments in the early days of Sunday football. Enough said!

Another well established Saturday League was struggling for member teams after the start of the Coventry and District Sunday Football League and the success of Coventry City FC. The Coventry Minor League was formed in 1926 as the Coventry J.O.C League (Juvenile Organising Committee). It was renamed the Coventry Minor League in 1945 and catered for Under-18 and Under-16 teams. Over a period of time the age restrictions were abandoned, and rebranded the Coventry Intermediate League. By 1965 the League was down to three teams excluding new applications, and at the AGM the Committee agreed to a transition to Sunday football, and again rebranded the Coventry and Central Warwickshire Sunday League. It shows that the League's committee have not shied away from change over decades. In recent years their membership has diminished and they face challenging times.

It was in this League that Barras Green WMC had some very successful seasons, winning Divisional Cups and successive promotions, in the mid-1970's.

Referees

Referees and Discipline are essential for amateur footballers. If the referee doesn't turn up for your game, the two teams have to decide whose representative will take the whistle. This can lead to confrontation, due to bias, and then players need to exercise discipline. Some sympathy must be shown to stand-in Referee, because he is doing the one job that no one else wanted to do!

The official Referee does not deserve sympathy; he is fully educated on the laws of the game, unlike the players. Some Referees, even in today's professional game, go out of their way to ensure that they make the headlines in the Sunday paper. Some Referees go about their work with quiet efficiency, and have discreet words in players ears, rather than blow his whistle for an offence and then run twenty yards away, beckoning the offending player to go to him. Some Referees are consistent in their reading and interpretation of offences, some are not, then the player loses his discipline.

The worst action that Referees take is in regard to retaliation, for instance a player in red tackles the player in blue with the ball from behind, taking the ball and both legs of the opponent, player blue reacts and confronts the player red. The Referee then books the player red for the tackle, and sends off player blue for violent conduct. Totally wrong! The Referee should send off player red and book player blue, on the basis that if the player red had tried to win the ball fairly, then player blue would not have had reason to confront player red. Enough said!

I would like to see Referees take a short time-out to consider the actions he is about to take, before brandishing any cards

From the outset of my footballing career, I resolved to play the game fairly, and not get involved with disputes on the field of play. I am quite level headed and easy going. However, football, even at grassroots level is a passionate and competitive game, and I was booked about fifteen times and sent off two.

Most of the bookings have been for arguing and/or foul and abusive language. This is something that I'm not proud of, I would rather be writing about my wonder goals, but in mitigation I am now going to describe what happened on some occasions.

My first booking came when I was playing for Moseley United. I had played as an emergency full back for the Reserves, and played well, and I was given my chance in the first team, due to an injury to the regular player. We were playing a Cup game in Leamington on a pitch behind the Potterton's Factory. There had been some frosts during the week and the ground was hard. Some games on municipal pitches had been called off. Our Referee agreed to play the match if we players took the conditions into account when tackling.

I had read my Jimmy Armfield "How to be a full back", in one of my Football Annuals, so I was well prepared for the task. My mate John, who was a first team regular by now, was playing wing half in front of me, so I had good cover. The game was competitive despite the conditions, and I was marking a speedy winger. I managed to contain him on several attacks, whilst settling into the higher tempo of first team football. After about half an hour, the winger received the ball in space, and charged forward. I think I caught him just below the knees and he skidded about ten yards on the frozen turf. The Referee had my name in the book before the winger had stopped sliding, and I was warned as to my future conduct.

My clean record had gone, and I sulked and moped, disappointed that I had a blemish on my short career. At half time, John gave me some comforting advice like "for f***s sake Derek, pull yourself together". I tried harder in the second half, but I had lost enthusiasm. The winger steered clear of me for the rest of the game, which we lost 1-0.

Other bookings followed on a regular basis, but only one other was due to a bad tackle. This was in a match between Moseley United first team and Stoke Aldermoor at Bubbenhall. We always had good games against the Aldermoor, and this game was no exception. During the second half I had made a run into the opposition half, and overrun the ball. I continued my charge and took their centre half's legs from under him as he took the ball away. His team mates were not very friendly toward me. "He dived" I said, but the referee had his note book out. I kept rambling on for a few minutes and he lost patience with me and took my name, at which point, I shut up. In hindsight I could have broken the Aldermoor player's leg!

The first sending off was in a Wickman Cup match at Yelverton Road. Brico Apprentices were playing Wickman Apprentices. This was the year after the Wickman team had lost in the final to Dunlop. The Apprentice Supervisor, Joe Williams, had laid the law down, saying that the Board of Directors wanted the Cup back at all costs. Before the game we heard that Brico were struggling to get a team together, and had included some Rugby Union players.

The game progressed and it became clear that the information was true as some of the Brico tackles were clumsy, and there was a quite a few hand-offs. The Referee overlooked these indiscretions, and then against the run of play Brico scored. In the second half, with our Supervisor's threats ringing in our ears, we equalised and then took the lead. Full time approached and I challenge for a high ball, the ball fell to the ground in front of me and my opponent, and as I made the clearance he attempted to charge down the ball, rugby style, my follow through caught him in the ribs. The Referee blew his whistle, and I expected the free kick for us, for obstruction. He sent me off for violent play! I was stunned.

The outcome of the match was a victory for Wickman, but the disgrace of having a player sent off for violent conduct was sufficient to remove them from the competition, and award the game to Brico. I had a reputation and there was a lot of talk behind my back at work for some time.

The second sending off was on one of Moseley United's trips to London. The travelling party included Frank Lyddieth, a Wickman colleague of Reg Kimber and a qualified Referee. Frank had offered to Referee the friendly match against a local team which was to take place in the morning. The game never flowed due to a strong wind and a bumpy pitch, and I felt that a lot of decisions were going against us. As the match progressed I was questioning Frank's decisions more and more. I knew him and I thought I could twist his arm a little bit. Anyway, I brought one of their players down with a late tackle, and Frank, sorry, the Referee sent me off for persistent infringement of the rules and foul play. Yes, he was probably right to do so. If he hadn't sent me off, I would have probably walked off any way.

I did walk off the pitch deliberately once when playing for Apollo Rangers. I was close to the end of my playing days, and a bit "couldn't care less". It was a nice day for football and we were playing a mediocre team, and winning comfortable. I had scored two goals including one direct from a corner, and I was urging the team on, but the other players became complacent and the opposition scored. I was appalled. We had used our substitute, but I threw a strop and walked off. Did anyone notice?

Well, yes the team manager did and he suspended me for two games. The second match was against my former team Barras Green WMC at Stoke Heath. I was gutted. I was ribbed by the Barras players, when they had heard about my suspension.

Bookings and Dismissals were supposed to be reported to the Birmingham County FA, which is the next tier up in the hierarchy that is the Football Association. Some Referees did not send in a report, for various reasons. Maybe, they thought that the booking during the game had diffused the situation, and no further action needed to be taken. Maybe, some Referees just didn't bother.

Players were fined and/or suspended by the BCFA, and if the offence suited, banned sine die (for life). Fines varied during my playing days from 5s0d (25p) to £2.50p. Suspensions for a dismissal, was normally four weeks. Only about four of my bookings were reported, but both of my dismissals were.

Despite everything, I always shook the Referee's hand at the end of the game. I also shook hands with opposing players. I learnt at an early stage in my life to grip hard the offered hand. Sometime you would shake hands with a limp wristed bloke; it was like strangling an eel!
The Secretaries of the teams had to see the Referees after the game to get the Match Card signed. Generally, the Referees were always polite, and prepared to discuss incidents calmly, no point in ranting and raving – the game was history!

A few of the local Referees made it onto the league list. Larry Watson, who played for Moseley United, was a good all round footballer, and took exams to become a Referee. He progressed through local leagues to Referee in the Football League. There are exceptions, but good footballers don't necessarily make good Referees. One of the reasons that you don't see ex-professional footballers wearing the black kit and a whistle, is that the years between retirement of the footballer and the retirement of the Referee, is too short to enable the chaps to gain the necessary experience.

In the Coventry and District League, there were some good Referees, John Loundon, Larry Riley, Kieran Barrett, Gordon Gear, Sid Bariball and Davy McLeod to name a few. They performed consistently well, were not arrogant, and took time to explain their decisions.

When playing for Avondale FC at Coundon Hall Park, the teams were huddled around the cast iron stove in the changing rooms at Waste Lane. The pitches were hard with a sprinkling of snow, and it was cold. The Referee turned up, ready changed, in an open necked short sleeved shirt. He gave us ten minutes to get changed!

One of the characters of local Refereeing was Mr Fenandes-Montez. His performances could be erratic, but he was likeable. He had a portly figure and wore long shorts over his knees, but he moved like a Matador – up on his toes, almost graceful, maybe it was his Spanish genes. The captain of Moseley United knew how to approach him. He would chat about the weather, and thank him for refereeing our game. We won – got all the decisions!

On one occasion, Mr Montez joined in the game for about ten seconds. He took the ball off one of our players, and dribbled the ball a few yards and passed the ball back to the player. We had all stopped and fell about laughing. He told us to "play on" as though nothing had happened. In another match, after half time, our goalkeeper ran to his goal and jumped up, to stretch his arms and body, and touch the crossbar. He jumped a little higher than he expected so he hung on the crossbar. Mr Fernades-Montez booked him! They broke the mould when he was born!

Cup Finals

We have all watched the FA Cup final on television, and the razzmatazz that goes with it. For the amateur footballer to play in a competition to win a sponsored trophy, such as the Coventry Telegraph Cup, or the Boyd-Carpenter Cup, means nothing, until they reach the final. The initial ties take place slotted in amongst the run-of-the-mill league programme, and offer them the chance to play against opposition from other football leagues in their area.

Each league will have their own Invitation Cup, whereby teams from the lower divisions have the chance to compete against supposedly stronger and more skilful teams in higher divisions. The beauty of the Cup competition is that all teams start on level terms.

I have been fortunate to play in two cup finals in the seasons 1973-74 and 1974/75 playing for the same team - Barras Green WMC. The Coventry Telegraph Minor Cup was for Saturday league teams and the final was played at the Courtaulds sports ground at Dovedale Road, Longford. The game was to be the last time that the Minor Cup would be contested. The Tom Cooke Memorial Cup is the Coventry and Central Warwickshire Sunday League cup and the final was played at The Butts.

Both finals were played at the end of hard seasons for both the Saturday and Sunday teams from Barras Green Working Mens Club. There had been a fixture jam due to bad weather, and the progress in all Cup competitions, and their success in winning the divisional titles of their respective league programs.

The Telegraph Minor Cup was an evening game, and the opponents were Clifton, Rugby. The Courtauld's ground was full size, and after playing on a parks pitch, both teams took time to adjust to the open spaces. I was playing full back and normally I would play a long ball up the touchline to the winger, but I had to advance twenty yards or so, to make certain my pass would reach. The game was even-steven for some time and then Clifton scored. The second half was similar to the first with no team on top. Manager John Pinnegar told Jack Foley, who had been playing as a stand-in centre half, to move up front and Bobby Halcrow to go to centre half. It was an inspired move as Jacko scored almost immediately to equalise. The game went into extra time. I was on the halfway line and didn't see our second goal in the gathering gloom, apparently substitute Grant Farquharson scored the winner. John

Pinnegar asked me to collect the Cup from the Coventry Evening Telegraph representative: a proud moment!

The players shared a communal bath, a novelty, and went back to the Barras Green Working Men's Club to celebrate the victory with their club members and supporters. I phoned Eileen from the club, to tell her of the team's triumph, and that I would be late home. She didn't understand – it's a man thing!

The Butts Arena in Spon End is now the home of Coventry Rugby Club. Before re-development it was a multi-purpose arena with a covered stand on one side of the site. The stadium catered for football, athletics, and cycling for which there was a banked track around the athletics track. The general public could use the facilities for training at a small cost. The first time I went there I walked out of the dressing rooms onto the banked track, and nearly got mown down by an irate cyclist!

The first time I had played at the Butts was for Wickman Apprentices in the Wickman Cup. The opposition was Dunlop, and they were organised. We were like a group of strangers. I was playing wing half, and I spent most of the game fetching the ball off the athletics track for throw-ins. We lost 6-1, embarrassing! Least said!

The Tom Cooke Memorial Cup was played on a Sunday morning, and Barras Green WMC had arranged transport to take the players and a host of supporters to the Butts.

The opposition was Newtown Athletic who we had beaten twice in league matches. Their team had different players to those used in the league games, but that's life! Again, the bigger pitch had an effect on the teams, and they chased the ball all over the park. That is apart from the opponent's right winger and me! The play was all up and down our right touchline, but their No7 was still hugging his touchline. My intention was to stay with him, but I also had to cover any mistakes in our defence, and as play went on I was drawn further in-field.

Manager John Pinnegar, kept shouting at me to stay out wide, I tried to explain what I was trying to do, but he insisted, so out I went. Bobby Halcrow scored for us, but as play continued, we were under more pressure around the penalty area, our keeper left the line in anticipation of a shot, and I went to cover the post as the ball suddenly flashed across the box straight to the incoming winger, I dashed out to tackle him but he side stepped me and lashed the ball into the net. Newtown scored later after another scramble in the box, but Jack Foley equalised before half time.

Early in the second half, Dave Buckingham scored after a mistake by their defence. The play was still mainly on our right, and the winger and I ran up and down the opposite touchline together, without seeing much of the ball. He went to play on the other wing for a while, during which time he scored his second goal, after a goalmouth scramble. Bobby Halcrow scored his second goal late on with a stunning strike, to win the game 4-3. Afterwards in the dressing room, one of our players wanted to know if I got the winger's phone number, "as you both looked happy together!"

I went for a shower and when I got back, everybody had disappeared, and the bus! I walked the two miles or so back to the Barras Green WMC. (I had left my money in the car). I was already two pints behind, but too knackered to catch up.

Injuries

Watching football on television today highlights the risk that players take every match. Injuries to professional footballers can cut short a lucrative career. The response by Trainers, and Ambulance and Medical staff has improved over the years, and the Physiotherapist is given a much better chance of healing the injury. The game today is much faster and the players more committed. Having said that, some of the fouls in the sixties and seventies, would make even the hardened player wince.

The world of the amateur footballer, was very different at that time, players didn't warm up before games, we used to get changed, have a cigarette, walk onto the pitch, put in a few crosses of the ball to stretch the goalie, and then perhaps a trot around penalty area, and we were fit and raring to go!

Football clubs were obliged to provide a medical kit, a bucket with cold water and a sponge, a whistle in case the referee didn't turn up, and a linesman. All amateur footballers were advised to get injury insurance – few bothered. The players of Works teams were covered by their firm's Industrial Accident policy, or so I was led to believe.

The pitches on which the games were played, could cause nasty injuries. My local park, Stoke Heath, was originally a landfill site. Amongst the rubbish dumped there, was a large quantity of glass, mainly broken bottles. Over the years due to settlement the glass had come to the surface. An elderly St John's Ambulance man and his young trainee assistants were kept very busy patching up bloodied legs and arms. The other problem with the glass bottles was that some of them were not broken, but complete and Victorian, a rare find! Some pitches had been excavated overnight by some idiot trying to "make a fast buck".

Other pitches around the Coventry area are laid on mine working spoil, Binley Fields being a good example. The Whitley common was used in the war to detonate live ammunition collected from the blitzed City, and surrounding areas. Seven Bomb Disposal servicemen lost their lives, when a 1000 lb Luftwaffe bomb blew up on the common, after they had transported it from the city centre. Unexploded ammunition is still being recovered across the city today. It makes you wonder!

Reg Kimber, in his capacity as Secretary of the Whitley Local History Group, wrote a book "Seven Brave Men", which records the events of that day, and traces the families of the servicemen.

At the final whistle, the game is over, and if you had an injury that a plaster, or aspirin could not heal, then you needed a Physiotherapist, who charged money for his services, kill or cure! Some clubs would pay all, or part of the costs, but generally you paid for the pleasure.

There were not many Physiotherapists in Coventry at that time, but I went to two during my playing days. The first was Stan Duncombe, his practice was near to the junction of Coundon Road and Moseley

Avenue, and I understand, he treated Coventry City and Coventry Rugby Club players.

I had injured my knee playing in an evening match at Bubbenhall for Moseley United reserves against YCW (Young Christian Workers). The pitch was hard and bare of grass down the middle, and I had stretched for a ball with my left leg, and somehow my right knee hit the ground hard. The kneecap was very sore and grazed, and I had a problem bending it to ride my motorbike home. It was very painful and stiff the next day, so I phoned Mr Duncombe for an appointment.

I had three half hour sessions with him. He applied heat to the joint, and then used a machine with electrodes to stimulate the muscles around the kneecap. The machine is used to breakdown the natural adhesions that the body forms when damaged. The body protects the area by producing fluid to cushion the damaged tissue. The Physiotherapist cannot treat and heal the damage with the fluid present, and must break down the adhesions to allow the body to absorb the fluid naturally. The knee responded quite well and as I was on a limited budget and it was the end of the season, I decided to let mother nature complete the healing.

The next time I went for treatment, I visited Mick Crossfield, who lived locally off Swancroft Road in Stoke Heath. He had a massive Alsatian type dog that was his doorkeeper and door bell! Only the hairs on the back of your neck moved, until he told the dog to "sit", only then could you enter. There was no brightly lit clinic, just a normal settee, covered in dog hair, but Mr Crossfield had basically the same equipment as Mr Duncombe. During your session the dog would circle the settee, eyeing up which limb he would go for if the chance arose.

The day before, I had played for Apollo Rangers against WMPTE (the Busmen) at the Municiple Sports Ground in Stoke Aldermoor. It was a cold and blustery day and I couldn't get warm. The pitch was heavy and the wind was affecting the game, but we were confident of a win. I was playing up front and jumped to head on a goal kick. The opposing centre half clattered into me and his knee caught me in the small of the back. That hurt. I tried to run it off but couldn't move quick or turn. We didn't have a physio on the line so I played on as best as I could. In hindsight I should have gone off and let the substitute have a game. Early in the second half, I again jumped to head the ball and landed awkwardly, the pain coursed down one leg. Time for the substitute!

Mick Crossfield checked my spine and hip joints and applied heat and used his machine in the damaged area. Finally he massaged the area and in his words "manipulated some muscle back into position". I played the next weekend, no pain or stiffness. Even today I get an ache in that area when I'm cold.

Years later, Eileen had a similar injury; her car had failed to start and having called the RAC, sat on the bonnet of the car for nearly two hours. It was a nice sunny day, but there was a chill in the breeze. Car fixed, she went home and we later went to do the weekly shop. As we loaded the car she picked up the heaviest bag and swung it into the boot. She couldn't walk the next day. I arranged a visit to the Abbey Clinic in Styvechale. I had been to see Carl Seal, the Physiotherapist for a non football injury, and had been pleased with the service. Carl checked Eileen's spine and breathing, again he applied some heat and massage to the back, repositioning muscle and Eileen skipped out of the clinic. Brilliant!

My apologies, I strayed from football related injuries. Head injuries are frequent in football and more so in rugby. The sight of bloodied heads is not pretty and if you have had stitches then you have some sympathy for the injured. Cuts can be repaired and leave a scar, but Concussion can leave the person with emptiness. I've had concussion and seen other players with it, and it isn't pleasant. For an amount of time, you are a zombie, your body is working fine, perhaps a bit unsteady, but you are talking, gibberish maybe, but you are not there and will have no recollection of some events of the day.

I was playing for Moseley United Reserves at Bubbenhall, and we were a man short. John, my mate, had arranged for his brother Mick to play. Mick was home on army leave and was making up for lost time. He didn't make it for kick-off but I remember him running onto the field during the game. The next thing I remember is waking up about four hours later. John had come to see how I was after my clash of heads during the game. Mum told him that I'd been asleep since he brought me home. I had a cold at that time but couldn't recall that, or anything about the previous week at work.

Ricky Bevan clashed heads when playing in another game at Bubbenhall for Moseley United Reserves. He played on after the injury as I had, but after the game, when we were getting changed, Ricky was chatting continuously, usually you could'nt get a word out of him. He kept repeating the same questions asking everyone in turn "Derek, did we win, what was the score?" He knew who we were, but there was a vacant look in his eyes, he wasn't there. When he arrived home his parents took him straight to hospital, and he stayed in overnight for observation, and was discharged the next day.

Apollo Rangers player, John Garner also suffered concussion, but not from a clash of heads. He was making one of his surging runs through midfield and pushed the ball just out of reach. The opponent was favourite to get the ball, but John stretched to block the ball against the other chaps legs. John's momentum carried him forward and he pivoted around the ball, so that he was facing the way he came, he flew yards landing on his back and his head hit the ground with a sickening thud. John was very fortunate that he didn't break his leg, but he had got concussion.

I had finished playing at that time and had taken daughter Wendy with me to feed the ducks on the canal, and wave to the barges as they came past. I could probably watch my former team mates as well! I had seen the injury and offered to take a groggy John to hospital. Somebody would collect his clothes from the changing rooms, and also contact his family.

With John securely belted in the front seat of my car, I had to take Wendy back home to Mum, which was on the way to A&E. As I was explaining to Eileeen what had happened, John was trying to get out of the car. He was half in and half out of the car entangled in the seat belt, trapped like a fly in a spiders web! (Eileen, Wendy and myself still have a chuckle about it, even now. Sorry John)

On arrival at the hospital, a Nurse recognised John's trauma and we were shepherded into a small room with a bed. We tried to make him comfortable, but he was still agitated and repeating his "where am I" questions. I told the Nurse what had happened and how he had landed. The A&E was quite busy and the Nurse said a doctor would be in to see him as soon as possible. After a while John settled down and drifted into sleep. The Nurse suggested that I could go if I wanted, and that his family was on the way. He was in good hands and so I went home.

You have heard the expression 'Break-a-leg', usually applied to actors prior to the first night of a new stage production. On the football pitch it can become a reality. I witnessed an unfortunate incident when playing for Barras Green WMC at Stoke Heath. Dave Buckingham broke both bones in his leg, in a collision with an opponent.

Dave was still a teenager, slight build, tall with long hair down his back. (It was the early seventies and everyone had long hair). Dave was a good centre forward and a regular goal scorer. Barras were on the attack and Dave, with the ball at his feet, took on the opposing centre half. The No5 was short and stocky and decided that he would break up the attack by whatever means possible. Dave dropped his shoulder and went to ghost past his opponent, the centre half blatantly stepped in front of him in a 'thou shall not pass' stance.

It was clear that Dave had a bad injury, and a spectator ran to the nearest phone box to call for an ambulance, while some of our players remonstrated with the guilty player. I sat with Dave for a while before the ambulance arrived, to try and keep him warm and reassure him, but he was in shock. The ambulance men expertly straightened his legs and encased the broken leg in an inflatable support. Dave was transported to hospital, and we resumed our match, but our thoughts were elsewhere.

Dave Buckingham resumed his playing career, but was out of the game for some time before his leg was strong enough. I had left the club when I next saw him play, but he hadn't regained his confidence at that time.

Football boots can become lethal weapons. It was bad enough in the days of leather studs. When they became worn, the nails holding them into the boot sole would be standing proud, and could be razor sharp. Adidas was probably the first company to manufacture boots with a multiple of studs in a moulded sole. These boots were also good for use on other surfaces, and were quite resilient. The new style boots were as comfortable as wearing shoes, and they had no toe caps as such. Cheaper imitations were soon on the market but suffered from bad stitching and soles that snapped in half. The professional players still yearned for a boot with a limited number of studs, and soon the screw-in stud was available.

The problem with this type of stud is that it is generally made of plastic, and it wears. Even on turf and composite surfaces – it wears. Players have to walk on concrete, paving slabs, and tarmac sometimes to reach the pitch. The head of the studs will burr over into a mushroom shape, the edge of which can be razor sharp!

Playing at Prior Deram Walk for Barras Green WMC in pouring rain on a heavy muddy pitch, I was playing at full back, and pushing forward with the ball, and as I evaded a challenge, I felt the opponents stud catch my ankle bone. For an instant I stopped to tell the chap how naughty he was, but the referee was waving play on, the attack fizzled out. I needed treatment as blood was spreading on my sock, which had been torn.

The skin was broken about an inch long, and we cleaned it as best we could, because my socks and boots were covered in blood. We wrapped some lint around the ankle to protect the cut, and I went to talk to the referee. We examined the opponent's boots, and sure enough some of the screw-in studs were badly worn. The referee asked the opponents team manager to remove all damaged studs in the boots, and then play continued.

The next day the ankle was very sore, bruised and swollen. I went to the doctors to get some antibiotics in case of infection. John Pinnegar, the Barras team manager arranged for one of the club members, Bill Delayburn to give me some treatment. Bill relied on heat and massage, no electrical probes for him, but was reluctant to apply heat around a healing cut. He applied his own mix of 'horse liniment' to the foot and the whole of the leg, and massaged it in. I went back every night that week, and as the scar healed the heat lamp was used, and more liniment and massage. It was three weeks before I played again. Thanks Bill.

Socialising

Moseley United Football Club had a good social side mainly due to the efforts of Honorary Secretary Reg Kimber. The players and committee used to meet on Tuesday nights to talk about the last weekend's games and select teams for the next matches. These meetings took place at the Stag Inn on the corner of Lamb Street and Bishop Street. It gave a chance for young players like John and I, seventeen at the time, to get to know the older players and learn how to improve our game.

The captains of the two teams would give a report on the games that had been played the weekend before, with open discussion afterwards. The Secretary would then tell the members about the fixtures for the forthcoming weekend, and explain meeting arrangements and/or transport to the ground. The team selection committee would then finalise the teams for those games. The formal side to the evening was closed with any other business.

Reg Kimber would organise Christmas nights out, wives and girlfriends invited. He arranged for us to go to the Castle Coffee House in Warwick, and hired a corporation double decker bus to take us there. I had been courting Eileen about two months at that time and John was accompanied by Pat, his soon-to-be wife, although I don't think he knew it at the time.

It was a bit of a tight squeeze in the restaurant, but the food was good and the beer was flowing. There was some short after dinner speeches. Reg had invited Bill Watts, the Match Secretary of the Coventry and District Football League, and a good speaker, who entertained us for some time.

The band started to play and some of the defenders were soon showing some good moves, on the dance floor. Eileen was quite shy at that time, and did not want to dance. I wasn't very good either, and we were still getting to know each other, so we found ourselves a quiet corner for most of the night. Aahh, loves young dream! The evening was a success and we were entertained further by Bill Watts, on the bus journey home.

The next Christmas event was held at the Higham Hall Hotel in Nuneaton, unfortunately it was instantly forgettable!

When Moseley United were using the pitch at the Bubbenhall Village playing field, we used the local facilities such as the Reading Rooms (A community meeting house, that also doubled as a Doctor's surgery), and the local pubs. The Rooms were used for changing into football kit, and the pub's toilets came in handy. In return we tried to support the local residents and traders.

The villagers would organise their annual Summer Fete, and ran a Donkey Derby in a bid to attract more visitors. Some of the players decided to have a ride, so I took all my leathers and crash helmet to wear. (I didn't take my motorbike – it was off the road again). I didn't know what to expect, but when it was my turn to ride behind the donkey, perched on a two wheeled buggy, I gripped the reins in one hand and clung onto the buggy frame with the other.

The flag went down and we were away, well almost. Donkeys are pack animals just like sheep, they have leaders and followers. My ass was a follower, but he was pretty quick as he chased after the boss donkey. It was quite hairy around the bumpy areas of the field but Dobbin carried me home in second place, some of the other donkeys were still grazing on the start line, carrots on sticks having no effect!

The landlady at the Malt Shovel pub, Mrs McNamara, was a vice-president of the football club, and Reg arranged a players' night out with food, quiz and raffles. It must have been on a Friday, and we were due to play the next day at Bubbenhall. The drink-drive laws did not apply in those days. The night went well, we all had a good laugh and a joke, plenty to eat and drink.

The next day, when we turned up for the game, one of the players was a bit sheepish, apparently he didn't feel to good when he left the pub and the fresh air hit him, anyway he got into his car and drove off into the dark country lanes. Somehow, he missed the sharp right hand turn just outside the village and ploughed through a hedge into someone's garden. Fortunately, he was alright, no broken bones, so he walked back to the village and called a taxi from the village telephone box. (No mobiles in the sixties). He returned in the morning and managed to recover his car. Very lucky chap!

Reg Kimber was good planner, he arranged for Moseley United to travel to London, play a match against a local team, hopefully about the same skill level as ourselves, and then watch Coventry City play their league match in the afternoon. The first such trip was before I joined the club, but Reg had managed to contact a team called Pantiles, and they were keen on the visit and had that weekend free. The Moseley United players travelled down by train and had a coach arranged to transfer them to the Pantiles ground.

The Pantiles football club was, I'm led to believe, a feeder club for the professional clubs in London, and therefore had some good players. Moseley United gave them a good game and won 4-3. The following year, we again won 4-3, but on the third trip, Pantiles had a fixture backlog and suggested that we contacted Leyton Orient FC, Coventry City's opponents the day of the trip. The O's were very accommodating and agreed to put out a team at their training ground!

The day arrived and we arrived at the training ground in good time, and were made very welcome. We had more than enough players for one team, so it was agreed that some people would have to play just one half. The game started and it soon became apparent to us that the opposition were good. The third goal went in within five minutes. Their trainer was apologetic and told his players to ease off, he also moved his players around so that they played out of position. By half time the score was 9-0, and with the change of players at half time, we thought we might be able to hold them. Their trainer liked the look of our centre forward, Stan Bradley, who despite the game being a bit one-sided, had given the Orient's defence some problems.

The trainer suggested that we swopped centre forwards, I don't think his player was very happy about it, but he agreed as did Stan. The second half commenced and the teams seemed fairly balanced. It was a good day for football and the game was over all too soon. Leyton Orient won 12-0 and Stan had scored a hat-trick against us. After a shower, we were treated to some sandwiches and drinks, and we said our goodbyes.

Leyton Orient FC had reserved us a block of seats at their Brisbane Road ground, for the second division match against our Sky Blues. The match was not a classic and resulted in a 1-1 draw. Then it was time for some food and a few pints to wash it down. Then back to Euston and home.

The whole experience was exciting for me. The first time I had been to London was when I was eleven, it was a school trip to the Houses of Parliament with a guided tour by the then MP for Coventry, Maurice Edelman. He was very patient with the sixty or so children from Holbrook school, but warned us not to sit on the seats in the House of Commons or the House of Lords, or we would be cast into the Tower of London. He said that there would be a small prize for the boy and girl who wrote the best essay about their trip to London and the Houses of Parliament. I was lucky to win that prize which was a book about the history of the Houses of Parliament. (I still have it). Thank you Maurice, you got my vote!

The next time I went to London was to attend the Machine Tool Exhibition at Olympia. A coach full of Wickman apprentices arrived with the specific instruction to find some equipment that would be of use to the Company to improve the quality and design of the Wickman products. I think we were in the Exhibition Hall thirty minutes, at the most. About half a dozen of us went to see the Cutty Sark at Greenwich then made our way back to Soho where we sampled some of the strip-tease joints. One of our group got separated from the rest, and was found later in a confused state, claiming he had been robbed. We were not very streetwise at that age.

Right where were we, yes! The next London trip for Moseley United FC was to coincide with Coventry City's fixture at Selhurst Park against Crystal Palace. The game was an evening kick off, so it was going to be a long day, and we would have to catch the Milk train home, which took longer to reach Coventry as it was diverted via Northampton. The Sky Blues were on target to get promotion to division one of the Football League. (No Premier League yet). Reg had managed to get us a game with a local team. The pitch was firm and the grass was sparse in places and long in other areas. There was a breeze down the pitch and the ball was bouncing all over the place. The opponents were quite aggressive considering it was a friendly match. It was a game of two halves, and we didn't get to grips with the pitch or the opposition. I got myself sent off late on in the second half. We lost the game 3-2.

After the game the group split up, some of the players had brought their wives with them, and wanted to go into central London. About a dozen of us caught the bus to Shepherds Bush and Loftus Road, where Queens Park Rangers were playing Scunthorpe. The journey across the City took a long time, and we arrived just after kick off.

QPR were way ahead in division three and were almost certain to be Division champions. Their team included Rodney Marsh and Stan Bowles, two enigmatic players of the decade, and both destined to play for England. The game was very one sided, and QPR ran out 5-1 winners and the crowd went home happy.

We made our way to Selhurst Park grabbing some food on the way. I was surprised by the terracing at the ground behind the goals it was very high, steep and full. The game was competitive and the Sky Blues earned a 2-2 draw, to keep them on course for promotion.

Reg Kimber introduced some school leavers from Whitley Abbey to the football club, and they gave the Reserve team a lift, the players were skilful and quick to adapt to adult football. The lads were enthusiastic and told their former schoolmates, who also wanted to play. It meant that the club now had a surplus of players for two teams. The matter was resolved and Moseley United Colts team was formed and entered into the Coventry and District League.

In their first season the Colts made good progress and surprised a lot of people. Some of the players were good enough to play in the First and Reserve teams; this was to cause some friction. The Colts team players wanted to stick together as a unit, but when clubs have First and Reserve teams, you have to play the better player in the First team.

About the same time Reg wanted to take the Colts to Holland to play in a tournament. I was not party to the discussions between the committee and Reg, but the outcome was that at the end of that season Reg Kimber resigned and took the Colts team and players with him. A sad day!

In the short time that I played for Parkstone WMC FC, a trip to Manchester was arranged with an overnight stay. This was almost like a Stag weekend for me, as I would be getting married in a couple of months time. The outing was primarily to watch Manchester City play at home against Sunderland. One of Parkstone's players, Doug Bryson, was born in Sunderland, so we agreed to support his team.

Manchester City had Tony Book as captain and full back. He was a late starter regarding his professional career and had played for England and was quite well respected. Under his leadership the team had been playing well and were in the top half of division one. Sunderland, on the other hand, had a young, promising side that was struggling at the bottom end of the table.

The match began with Man City stretching the Black Cats defence. Sunderland however, appeared to have a match plan, and that was to attack Tony Book as much as possible. Poor Tony, he wasn't the quickest of players, and he found himself up against two or more opponents. We, as temporary enrolled Sunderland supporters, cheered and jeered him everytime he was beaten, tackled, or dispossessed, or blew his nose. We booed and chanted and by the end of the game were hoarse. The Manchester fans were also booing their demoralised team. Sunderland who were odds on to lose, rose to the occasion and battled for every ball against a better team, and overcame them, winning 1-0.

Sunderland captain Ces Irwin, a giant of a man, ran over to us at the final whistle to applaud us, and we applauded him and his team. That night, in the pub, we watched Match of the Day and were surprised how our vocal support had drowned out the Man City supporters. In the morning after breakfast, we had a twenty five a side football match in the local park in normal shoes and clothes. After a few more drinks in the local Working Mens Club (Affiliated), we caught the bus home.

Apollo Rangers FC also had trips to the Manchester area. The day trip by coach was to Haydock Park horse racing course, with a visit to a Steak House and trendy pub afterwards. I'm not a horse racing person, or a betting man (the Grand National excepted), but don't knock it until you've tried it.

The first visit I made was the second for other players, and they were still talking about the last one, especially the trendy pub. The trip up was uneventful and we pulled into Haydock Park, it was a cold, overcast day and I got the feeling that, either the meeting had been called off, or that other punters were waiting for the sun to shine. There was a distinct lack of spectators, but the horses did eventually show their faces and other things, was that a stallion or a gelding?

I soon got into the routine whereby you queue for a beer, you drink your beer, you go to a bookie and give him a pound, you find a good vantage point in the covered stand, you watch the race, you tear up your betting slip, then repeat the whole thing again eight times. Oh, and go to the toilet as well!

I'm sure that the donkey I rode at the Bubbenhall village fete was running in the second race. It wasn't a profitable experience for me but some of the lads won. In the evening we found the Steak House, and fed and watered moved onto the trendy pub. It seemed to be suffering from the same malaise as Haydock Park.

On the previous visit, the pub was rocking and you couldn't get to the bar, which was full of classy birds, not parrots, young and lovely things. Tough – I was married now. Anyway, back to reality, the place was dead, but we had a drink and another and the pub filled up a little, but still no sign of the pretty young things. I think I must have caught a chill at the races, so I went to sleep on the back seat of the coach. I should have had couple of Port and Brandies to warm me up.

The next year, Haydock Park was totally different, bright sunshine, warm breeze, and thousands of punters. I've never seen so many coaches, if you placed them end to end, you could reach the moon. They were parked row upon row, bumper to bumper. The stands were packed, the bars overwhelmed, and the toilets overflowing. If you queued for a drink, you missed a race.

Apparently, it was big race day, probably on par with Aintree, Ascot, Epsom and Cheltenham. After the last race, we made our way back to our coach, somewhere in the middle of the forest of coaches. By some miracle our coach was full within twenty minutes of the last race, but we had to wait for the coach jam to clear. We eventually made our way to our 'favourite' pub to finish off the day, at least we knew that we would be able to get to the bar!

Laundry

Grassroots football teams provide all, or some of the kit, and during the games the shirts, shorts and socks take quite a hammering. Grass stains and gritty mud damage the material, but with the wonder of modern washing powders, the kit can be regenerated back to its spotless condition ready for the next weekend's fixtures. Some teams had the funds to have their kit laundered, but there was always the chance that the kit wouldn't be ready in time, or that some of the kit had been lost amongst other laundry.

Generally, it was down to the wife of one of the players to wash the dirty linen. Sometimes, the players would take it in turn to get the kit washed at home; it didn't always go down very well with the lady of the house. It wasn't so much the washing of the kit, but the drying. In the 1960's not everyone had a washing machine, some households still relied on the washtub, dolly and mangle. Even the new Hoover twin tub that we bought in 1970, when we got married, would never have coped with load of kit. The machine would have been for two days non stop!

Perhaps it was just a case of taking the whole heap of muddy shirts, shorts and socks down to the local Laundrette, with the family washing. Having said all that, it was a spectacular sight to see a row of twelve shirts, all in numerical order, on the clothes line blowing in the wind, on a sunny Monday morning.

My thanks go to all the ladies who carried out this unenviable task, week in week out, during the football season. I know that some teams used to send an annual gift to the domestic goddess's who looked after the kits with care and professionalism, and by God they deserved it.

Part 4 Press Reports

The Coventry Evening Telegraph produced a weekly sports edition on a Saturday evening called 'The Pink'. The number one subject was football and in particular Coventry City Football Club. However, Coventry also had an excellent Rugby Football Club, and in Warwickshire County Cricket a formidable eleven in the County Championship. So called minority sports, golf, darts, bagatelle, snooker, boxing, hockey, bowls etc., were all well covered by 'The Pink'.

CCFC took up many columns in the paper, from match day reports direct from the game by correspondent Nemo, League results and tables, in-depth analysis of the teams form, and player cameos. Local non-League clubs, Nuneaton Borough, Bedworth Town, Rugby Town and Lockheed Leamington had their own sections.

Junior, or Amateur football referred to grassroots football played locally on works and parks pitches. For the amateur footballer, 'The Pink' was their only way of finding out how their team was doing compared to others in their division. Most weeks there would be a comprehensive list of results from the previous weeks games, and a summary of the action from some the games. If you had scored a hat trick, you might get your name in 'The Pink'!

A lot of hard work went into producing these summaries, and it was dependant on the football club's secretaries, sending in their match cards on time, to their League's Match Secretary. Both the home and away teams had to complete a match card. As well as the team players names, the card had space for comments about the game, and there was a box where you could mark the referee. The Referee had to sign the card and he could add his comment if he wanted to. The cards had to be posted immediately after the game. Club Secretaries were encouraged to telephone their match result into the Telegraph, if only to fill in column space or the Stop Press!

The League Match Secretaries could then sort through the cards formulating the results into divisions and updating tables, and then sift through the reports to find outstanding results, top scorers, and facts of interest. This information would then be passed on to the Coventry Evening Telegraph. The Sports Editors would compose the pages using as much of the summaries from all the Leagues, dependant on column space.

In the early sixties, all this work was done in time for the Wednesday edition. That was incredible when you consider that they had to rely on the post, and everything was handwritten and the newspaper had to build up plates for the presses to print the story. Nowadays, the post is unreliable and we have computers to do the hard work.

The fixtures for next weekend's games would appear in the Thursday edition for the Saturday matches and Friday edition for Sundays.

'The Pink' regularly included match reports of local games. Leagues would have representatives who would attend the chosen fixture, and obtain the names of both sets of players prior to kick off. He would then take notes on the first half action, and telephone in his report from a nearby phone box (no mobile phones in those days). He would return and watch the rest of the match and again phone in his report. Generally the article in 'The Pink' would have a good description of the first half action, but rarely anything about the second half, except the final result, and sometimes that would appear in the Stop Press on the back page.

The 'Reporter' for the Coventry and District Football League was usually Cyril Stafford, or occasionally Bill Watts, when he hadn't got a game to referee. They were on the committee of the league and together with Fred Hefford the Match Secretary, were genuine, friendly people, and well respected. Fred was a teacher at my old school Foxford. He chain smoked continuously, and I always wondered how he coped without a cigarette during class time.

A new feature in 'The Pink', called the "Star Junior Match" appeared in the late 1960's. The Telegraph Reporter, Frank Thomas, and a cameraman, would turn up and take photographs of both teams, and then make a full report of the match. In 'The Pink' that night, the complete report would fill at least a column, and there would be an action photograph. Moseley United was one of the teams to feature, in a fixture against Hen Lane Social. I was pleased to have my name mentioned five times, but spelt wrong once! Interesting reading forty years later

Here are some paragraphs that appeared in 'The Pink', relevant to the teams that I played for.

Moseley United 1963/64 to 1969/70

14.09.1963   Moseley United Reserves had a forward line in which every player was aged under 17, and in fact did very well. A late slump saw them lose 5-0 to Sherbourne Reserves. Outside left Parkes hit a Hat-trick.

19.10.1963   Moseley United v Unbrako Reserves.
Freeman the Moseley keeper was kept busy with lively thrusts by the Unbrako attack. At the other end Miller saved well from Whitmore and Janes. Walker sent Unbrako into the lead in the 25th minute, and Biggers nearly increased the lead, but Freeman saved well from close range. Unbrako kept up the pressure for the rest of the half.
Half time: Moseley United 0   Unbrako 1
Unbrako cinched the match with second half goals from Beaufoy, Butler and Walker. Whitmore replied for Moseley
Full time: Moseley United 2   Unbrako 4

18.01.1964   Moseley United gained their first success of the season when they defeated fellow strugglers Tile Hill Old Boys. Tile Hill took took the lead with a penalty converted by their goalkeeper, Goodall. Determined pressure, brought goals from Setchell and Farquhar for Moseley.

18.01.1964   Moseley United Reserves won the battle of the bottom clubs 2-0, thanks to two early goals against Brinklow United.

25.01.1964   Tile Hill take over the wooden spoon from Moseley United who won for the second successive week. Goals from Farquhar (2) and Colledge gave Moseley a 3-2 victory over Baginton British Legion.

25.01.1964   Moseley United with outside left Watson, converted from goalkeeper, netting the goals that defeated Whoberly 2-1.

15.02.1964   Lowly Moseley United Reserves managed to defeat Avondale 9-2. Bradley and Whitmore both had hat-tricks here.

22.02.1964   Hastings, despite reaching double figures, did not have things all their own way against lowly Moseley United. Their opponents with Bradley again on the hat-trick mark, managed to score four times for the first time this season. Centre forward Summerfield (5) and fellow forward Watts (3) led the Hastings goal rush.

07.03.1964   Bottom club Moseley United, making a valiant effort to escape relegation, pipped St. Lukes 4-2, but they stay at the foot of the table.

07.03.1964   Veasey and Sharples with ten men, deserved their 2-1 victory over Moseley United Reserves.

12.09.1964   Moseley United, relegated last season, and determined to regain their First Division place as quickly as possible, made a splendid start in the second by whipping Allesley Park 8-0. Bradley, Janes and Farquhar scored two apiece and Whitmore and Setchell one each.

03.10.1964   Boyd Carpenter Cup matches
             Moseley United v Beechwood Reserves
Beechwood were two up at half time, but after the interval goals from Bradley (2), Janes and Farquhar put Moseley in the lead. Beechwood retaliated and reduced the deficit, but Whitmore made the issue safe for

Moseley with a fine goal. The Moseley Reserve team however, were knocked out quite easily by Pinley CC who scored six without reply. When Pinley scored the first goal, the ball hit a motorcycle parked behind the goal and burst. The game ended with Moseley missing a penalty and their right back conceding an own goal.

17.10.1964   Benevolent Cup 1st Round
              GEC v Moseley United

Opening play favoured Moseley with Janes and Farquhar going close. Keeping up the pressure a combined movement ended with Janes shooting over when well placed. Freeman saved brilliantly from Toogood and later saved a dangerous situation diving at the feet of Hall. Farquhar hit the upright for Moseley with a good effort, and in further attacks Willis and Freeman were prominent by safely dealing with all scoring efforts.
Half Time: GEC 0 Moseley United 0
Bradley and Farquhar scored for Moseley and Hall for GEC.
Full Time: GEC 1 Moseley United 3

09.01.1965   Moseley United with several games in hand, took both points from Unicorn Celtic. With most of their injured players now fit again, Moseley will take some stopping in this division. It was nice to see Derek Langford back in goal for them after an absence of 12 months.

09.01.1965   Veasey and Sharples fielded a depleted side for their match with Moseley United Reserves and were beaten 8-2. Watson (4) and Hewitt (3) were top scorers.

06.02.1965   Young Steve Whitmore again scored a couple for Moseley United, and with further goals from Farquhar and Sanders they had a comfortable win over Allesley Park, who failed to pierce the Moseley defence. Moseley are four points behind Howitzers, but have five games in hand.

06.02.1965   Full back Reg New of Moseley United Reserves has recently been tried as a centre forward, and it is paying dividends for he notched his first hat-trick against Tile Hill Reserves, so helping his side to victory.

27.02.1965   Another four goal forward was Hewitt of Moseley United Reserves, who easily accounted for a weakened Sherwyn Albion Reserves. Reg Kimber at left back, came upfield to hit one of the nine goals – his first for a very long time!

06.03.1965   After a goalless first half, Moseley United took a further twenty minutes before they pierced the St. Lukes Reserves defence, and this was from the penalty spot. Janes, who scored again later to give Moseley a two clear goals victory, but the young Saints made them fight all the way. This win puts Moseley United on top of the league for the first time.

06.03.1965   Queen Margarets won against Moseley United Reserves by 7-2. Moseley were leading 2-1 at the interval, but they were clearly upset by some of the referees decisions. It is unfortunate every game cannot be taken by an official referee, but we sometimes have to ask others to perform this onerous task.

10.04.1965   Moseley United on their club outing to London, played Pantiles FC, unbeaten this season. Their opponents include most of the London professional colts teams, but this did not deter Moseley, who played their best game of the season and built a 4-1 lead by half time. Feeling the strain, Moseley conceded another two goals, but finished up worthy winners.

01.05.1965   In Division 2, Moseley United already assured of top place, expected to gain another two points, but Unicorn Celtic surprised them by giving as good a display as any team Moseley have played this season. Moseley built up a two goal lead only for Unicorn to equalise before half time. The same pattern was repeated in the second half, and all voted it the best League game of the season. Farquhar scored all the home teams goals, bringing his total up to 38 for the season, the best effort by a Moseley forward for many seasons.

06.11.1965   With a comfortable 9-2 win over pointless Balsall, Moseley United took over the leading position in Division 1. Steve Whitmore registered his third hat-trick and Lambert making his first team debut, also scored. Alan Setchell, the Moseley right winger, is now at Sheffield University and his many friends will be delighted to hear he has been chosen for his University First XI.

20.11.1965   President's Cup 1st Round.
Moseley United, entertaining Exhall Rangers, did most of the pressing and were four goals up at half time, with goals by Vallely and Janes (3), but Exhall fought back well enough to record goals from Evans, Sibley and Lewis. Moseley retaliated with another Bradley goal to make the issue safe.

04.12.1965   Thanks to a goal scored three minutes from the end, Fillongley gained two points from their clash with Moseley United. As one could expect from two teams striving for Division 1 honours, the game proved exciting; in fact Moseley reported it as one of the best this season. John Colledge, at wing half for the losers, played another magnificent game.

04.12.1965   Despite their 9-0 defeat, the Brassworkers Reserves played very well until the last twenty minutes, when their defence cracked under severe Moseley United Reserve attacks. When Brassworkers have played together a few times, they will be a force to be reckoned with. Pat Mahon, the Moseley half back had a splendid game and was credited with a hat-trick.

18.12.1965   Unicorn Celtic v Moseley United.
In a Moseley attack, Vallely put just over the bar. After 15 minutes a blunder by the Moseley defence let in R.Eardman to give Unicorn the lead. After twenty minutes a good pass from Vallely found Lindop to make the scores level. Five minutes later Mahon put Moseley in front. In another Moseley attack Millward made a grand save from Setchwell and after 40 minutes Colledge scored No.3 for Moseley
Half time: Unicorn Celtic 1 Moseley United 3
Unicorn were soon on the attack and Wilding took advantage of another defensive blunder and reduced the lead, and just after he made the scores level. In a Moseley attack Bradley scored. Fifteen minutes from time Wilding made the scores level again, and just after Jones put Celtic in front.
Full time: Unicorn Celtic 5 Moseley United 4

08.01.1966   Moseley United Reserves were another promotion prospect to suffer badly, as Avondale, profiting by defensive mistakes, went into a two goal lead and then rubbed it in by slamming in three goals in the first five minutes of the second half to put the issue beyond all doubt.

15.01.1966   Moseley, already suffering from injuries to four first team regulars, suffered another blow on Saturday when their skipper Bert Ottley broke a leg. Moseley were leading 2-1 at the time of the accident. Despite the handicap, Moseley forged ahead, when Setchell making a rare appearance, hit in two further goals. The extra effort, however, told in the second half when Howitzers hit back fiercely to level the scores. Bradley showed some of his real shooting ability by adding another two goals to bring his match total to four.

05.02.1966   Meadway Rovers, leaders in Division 1 of the District League, were made to go all out by Moseley United before running out winners by 5-3 Moseley had most of the play in the first half and goals by Bradley, Janes and Colledge gave them a 3-1 lead, T.Smith having scored for Meadway. Meadway pressed strongly but it was not until twenty minutes from time they gained the upper hand, and won the points with a goal from T.Smith and a Fletcher hat-trick.

05.02.1965   At half time, Jubilee Athletic were leading Moseley United Reserves by 3-0, and were not even worried by having missed a penalty. What a transformation in the second half as a Moseley revival resulted in goals from Lambert (2), Hart (2) and Hempshall. Although Jubilee fell away after this onslaught, they rallied sufficiently to reduce the deficit by one more goal.

10.09.1966   Sharp shooting Setchell scored four goals in Moseley United's 8-2 victory over Howitzers in the First Division of the Coventry District League. Parsons netted two, and Colledge, captain for the day, scored and also had an outstanding game at right half

15.10.1966   FC Olympic had enough chances to be well in front at half time against Moseley United Reserves, but after a goalless first half the Moseley lads rubbed it in by slamming in five goals in the second half. Hewitt, Lindop (2) and Mahon (2) doing the damage.

29.10.1966   The match of the day in Division 1, that between Clarkson's Sports and Moseley United ended fittingly in a 3-3 draw after a hard and well fought game. L.Watson, playing his first game for the senior side scored two goals.

12.11.1966   A month ago, Moseley United beat Tile Hill O.B. by a solitary goal, and the return game was just as close. After Moseley had established a 1-0 interval lead, the Old Boys equalised, but a great solo effort by Colledge resulted in a second goal for Moseley.

03.12.1966   Meeting their chief rivals for District League honours, St.Lukes showed a return to their best form when they beat Moseley United 6-3 in a Division 1 match. The Saints right winger was in great form and netted a hat-trick. Colledge scored Moseley's three, two from the penalty spot.

21.01.1967   Folly Lane v Moseley United
After 20 Minutes Folly Lane took the lead, Dean scoring from close in. Good work by the Moseley forwards ended with Hempshall putting the ball past Croker to make the scores level. Just before half time Freeman made a good save from Mitchell.
Half time: Folly Lane 1 Moseley United 1
Mitchell scored for Folly Lane in the second half.
Full time: Folly Lane 2 Moseley United 1

04.02.1967   Watch Fillongley, however, for another fine win over Moseley United puts them in a good position and at the moment they are playing as well as anyone. Sharples scored two goals again for Fillongley and Vallely was prominent for Moseley. Stan Bradley, the Moseley leader, who has been such a fine club player, is shortly emigrating to Australia, and this was his last game.

04.02.1967   Moseley United v St.Lukes
Moseley's initial attack saw a close range shot by Vallely rebound to safety off the crossbar. After a period of defensive play the visitors came more into the game and Sigsworth went close on two occasions. In another Moseley attack a drive from Watson cannoned off the crossbar. The last kick of the opening half saw the crossbar come to the visitors rescue from a Colledge shot.
Half time: Moseley United 0 St.Lukes 0
In a well contested second half, a header by Miller gained St.Lukes the points.
Full time: Moseley United 0 St.Lukes 1

18.02.1967   Barras Green registered their best victory this term when hammering Moseley United Reserves 0-9.

01.04.1967   Moseley United game had a familiar result - won by the odd goal - but for once it was in Moseley's favour. It was a poor game against Sherwyn Albion spoilt mainly by that high wind, but Moseley will not mind that having won 2-1.

02.09.1967   Moseley United v Saunders Hall
Both sides attacked in turn although neither goalkeeper was troubled due to poor finishing. After twelve minutes Hewitt put the home side in the lead, beating Evans with a fine ground shot. Saunders Hall equalised against the run of play when Neil shot through a packed goalmouth after an indirect free kick. A few minutes later, the same player should have given his side the lead but shot over.
Half time: Moseley United 1 Saunders Hall 1
Full time: Moseley United 2 Saunders Hall 2

21.09.1967   Moseley United Reserves came from behind twice to snatch a point from St.James Reserves. St.James were soon two goals ahead, but Moseley rallied strongly before half time and Larry Watson put them on terms with two close range shots. Fifteen minutes from time St.James went ahead and just when it looked as if they would hold onto their slender advantage full back Bevan popped up with a last minute equaliser.

07.10.1967   Moseley United v Sherwyn Albion
Sherwyn took the initiative and the Moseley defence gave away two corners from which Forster headed narrowly over from the first and East over again from the second. Mahon made a good run and from his pass Wall had his shot turned round by MacDonald for a corner. Then West hit the underside of the crossbar before Colledge put Moseley ahead with a Sherwyn defence hesitant. MacDonald was now repeatedly in action saving brilliantly from Colledge and Wall, but was beaten by Wall from a pass by West to increase Moseley's lead.
Half time: Moseley United 2 Sherwyn Albion 0
Full time: Moseley United 5 Sherwyn Albion 2

04.11.1967   Kenilworth WMC v Moseley United
              Telegraph Junior Cup

Kenilworth started strongly, mounting attack after attack, but the efficient play of Bevan and Mahon in the visitors defence kept them ahead. When Moseley settled down, they displayed the finer touches with Wall and West using the ball well. Hempshall put the visitors into the lead with a shot that completely deceived Young in the home goal. In a goalmouth scramble Parsons added the second goal for Moseley. The visitors were doing all the attacking and the home defence was under heavy pressure. Bevan added the visitors third with a fine shot.
Half time: Kenilworth WMC 0 Moseley United 3
Jones and O'Malley scored for Kenilworth and Wall and Williams for Moseley
Full time: Kenilworth WMC 2 Moseley United 5

29.11.1967   Stoke Aldermoor missed a good opportunity to join the top teams when they went down to Moseley, a team that has been losing consistently by one goal margins. Moseley, for whom West scored a magnificent goal, won 2-1.

20.12.1967   Happy days for Moseley United Reserves – they won their first match of the season. It seemed as though they were heading for defeat again when Reid gave Henley College the lead but Whitmore and Twigg gave Moseley the points.

03.01.1968   Moseley United were hit by 'flu and started with ten men. Not surprisingly they were on the defensive, but held out for twenty minutes before Stevens scored for the Aldermoor. Then, Corrigan the Stoke 'keeper, did well to stop drives from Wall and Whitmore, before Hempshall levelled the scores. In an exciting last half Stevens the home right winger, netted again to clinch victory.

14.02.1968   Five goals from right winger Vallely enabled Moseley United Reserves to beat Leofric Reserves 6-0. Bert Ottley, making his first appearance since breaking a leg, played a great part in the Moseley defence.

28.02.1968   Avondale entered the semi-finals for the first time. Avondale scored twice in the first half against Moseley United Reserves and went on to win 3-1. Adams, the winner's leader, was prominent, scoring two of his side's goals.

13.03.1968   The other relegation-battling outfits, Moseley United and St.Lukes, clashed at Bubbenhall with Moseley coming safely through 5-1. Wall got a hat-trick.

20.03.1968   Mary Magdalen were fortunate to gain a 2-2 draw with Moseley United Reserves. Fortunate because their second goal came from a clearance which was carried on the wind and dipped under the bar, although Moseley claimed it went over the goal. (No nets)

11.04.1968   Moseley United eased their relegation worries slightly by beating Unicorn Celtic 2-1. Harrington and Williams were the Moseley marksmen.

05.10.1968   Moseley United Reserves, who managed only two wins all last season, have reached that figure already this term by beating Henley College Reserves 3-2.

02.11.1968   It was a good day for Moseley United. All their teams collected maximum points, with the first team knocking Stoneleigh out of the Boyd Carpenter Cup, the Reserves beating YCW Reserves by three goals, and the Colts beating Copsewood 5-2. Goode got a hat-trick in that clash.

16.11.1968   Moseley United drew 3-3 with Sherwyn Albion. Vallely scored a hat-trick for Moseley from the centre forward position, and Goode grabbed a hat-trick for Moseley Colts in their 7-2 victory over Homefire Reserves.

07.12.1968   Adams the Avondale leader was in a goal hungry mood against Moseley United Reserves and scored a hat-trick in his side's 5-0 victory.

07.12.1968   Birmingham County Youth Cup
Moseley United Colts v Warwickshire Club Kings.
Goode scored for Moseley after twenty minutes from a cross by Steane. Starling twice put the ball over the bar when played through, but play was generally even. Beasley prompted his forwards well, but United's hard tackling denied the visitors many scoring chances. Simpson was often in action in the visitor's goal.
Half time: Moseley United Colts 1 Warwickshire Club Kings 0
Full time: Moseley United Colts 2 Warwickshire Club Kings 1

11.01.1969   Birmingham County Youth Cup
Khasla Sports v Moseley United Colts
Moseley United Colts are the pride of Coventry and District League. They reached the semi-final of the Birmingham County Youth Cup by beating Khasla Sports, Smethwick 4-0 away from home. Doyle and Boston shot Moseley into the lead and two goals within the last ten minutes from Goode sealed the issue. This is Moseley's ninth consecutive win and their manager Reg Kimber says: "The team have really matured since the start of the season and feel confident that they can now reach the final of the Youth Cup.

03.03.1969   Coachmakers v Moseley United.
Boston in the Moseley goal was soon in action saving from Cook and Bennett. Moseley then took up the attack and Simpson saved at full length a hard drive by East. Coachmakers were soon back on the attack

and Boston was again prominent in saving in quick succession from Duggan, but later was beaten by Barber following a corner. Soon after, Bennett faced with an open goal, put wide of the upright. Coachmakers continued to have the better of the exchanges, but offside spoiled many good moves.
Half time: Coachmakers 1 Moseley United 0
Cook and Rawbone scored for Coachmakers in the second half
Full time: Coachmakers 3 Moseley United 0

03.03.1969   Birmingham Youth Cup - Semi-Final
             St. Francis Xavier v Moseley United Colts
In one of Moseley's attacks, Minchin saved from Morris. After ten minutes St. Francis took the lead, Paget giving Stacey no chance from close in. Five minutes later Jones gave Goode a grand pass and he went on to level the scores. In another Moseley attack Steane hit an upright with the goalkeeper well beaten. At the other end Stacey made a fine save from Morris.
Half time: St. Francis Xavier 1 Moseley United Colts 1
Full time: St. Francis Xavier 1 Moseley United Colts 2

12.04.1969   A Benefit match involving a Celebrity XI is to be organised for 17-year-old Brian Doubleday, whose promising football career was tragically ended when he had is left leg amputated below the knee after a motor cycle accident. Brian, a member of the Moseley United Colts team which has reached the final of the Birmigham County Youth Cup, is expected to be in hospital for three months. Brian is a member of the Whitley Rangers cycle speedway team, and was rated one of the top 16 cycle speedway riders in the country after reaching the finals of the National Senior Championships.

10.05.1969   Birmingham County Youth Cup – Final
             Moseley United Colts v Chelmsley Town
The Moseley goal was under constant pressure in the opening stages and Stacey was kept busy, Barker was in a good position to give

Chelmsley an early lead when Stacey missed a cross from Quirk, but with the goal open, he shot wide. Chelmsley forced two successive corners but were unable to take advantage, Moseley scrambling the ball away. Moseley came more into the game, and Wild was tested on two occasions. On the half hour, a long ball down the wing found Goode, who without hesitation, shot on the turn and easily beat Wild. Barker levelled for Chelmsley five minutes later, when he headed in from a corner. A minute late Moseley went in front again, Goode again being on target. Page levelled for Chelmsley from the penalty spot
Half time: Moseley United Colts 2 Chelmsley Town 2
Full time: Moseley United Colts 3 Chelmsley Town 4

18.10.1969   Moseley United used the offside trap to great effect in a goalless draw against Whitnash.

08.11.1969   President's Cup 1st Round.
                       Tile Hill O.B. v Moseley United
Tile Hill Old Boys were soon on the attack, and Mahon did well to clear off the line, and in another attack Mistear put over the bar. At the other end Randall made a good save from East. Tile Hill had a chance to take the lead, but the forwards were too slow and Evans cleared off the line. Tile Hill were putting on the pressure and Evans made good saves from Cox and Birchall. After thirty minutes the Old Boys took the lead when Luxton beat four defenders to put the ball in the corner of the net. Three minutes later Moseley united equalised when Bevan scored from close in. After forty minutes a long ball from Farquhar found Bevan who ran on to put the ball past Randall and Moseley into the lead.
Half time: Tile Hill Old Boys 1 Moseley United 2
Full time: Tile Hill Old Boys 2 Moseley United 4 (Bevan hat-trick)

06.12.1969   Moseley United, despite being a man short and a goal down after two minutes, in their Coventry and District League game against Meadway, mastered the difficult ground conditions to win 4-2.

Hempshall, Vallely and Farquhar (2) netted for the winners and Hall and Tompkins replied.

06.12.1969   Hen Lane recorded the highest score of the season with a 0-16 victory over struggling Moseley United Reserves, who only had nine men. Margaret (3), R Nicholls (3) and D Nicholls (2) were Hen Lane's top marksmen

13.12.1969   Star Junior Match by Frank Thomas
Moseley United 1 Hen Lane Social 2

Moseley United have a reputation for sporting play, but have yet to win any major honours in the Coventry and District League, After winning through from the Third to the First Division they have usually finished in a mid table position. Hen Lane formerly known as St.Luke's, assumed their present name after being relegated to the Second Division two seasons ago. Once winners of the President's Cup, Hen Lane were soon promoted again and hold a position in the top half of the First Division.

Moseley United: Bowes, Pearce, Harrington (M), East, Mahon, Bevan, Harrington (P), Farquhar, Hempshall, Parsons, Vallely.

Hen Lane Social: Clifton, Brook, Bray, Gordon, Hammersley, Puffett, Nichols (R), Preece, Nichols (D), Davies, Bird.

Referee: Mr W Warner.

Moseley took up the attack from the kick off with Hempshall shooting just wide with a twenty-five yard effort. A poorly taken free-kick by the homesters gave Hen Lane possession but Nichols (D) ran offside to spoil a good chance. A good pass by Bevan put Hempshall away and the winger's shot was turned round the post by Clifton. From the resultant corner East headed inches high. in another home attack good work by Parsons gave Vallely an opening only for the inside man to shave the upright with a good shot.

After twelve minutes Hen Lane took the lead, when Hammersley found Nichols (R) with a good pass and from the wingers cross, Bird dived to head into the net. Hen Lane missed a great chance to increase their lead when Bird raced through to present Nichols (D) with an open goal, but the centre forward slipped and put the ball outside. Moseley's defence was put in trouble when Bowes was penalised for carrying but Bevan headed clear off the goal line, when Bray's free-kick was deflected.

Hen Lane, moving the ball quickly, were the more dangerous side and again Bevan saved his side heading away a free-kick by Puffett and in another attack Nichols (D) was adjudged offside when Nichols (R) broke through.

Moseley took play to the other end with a neat passing move only for Valley to finish weakly, when presented with a good chance by Hempshall. Bird was proving a dangerous raider and from one of his breaks Nichols (R) just failed to reach the ball with the goal wide open. A free-kick from just outside the penalty area nearly brought the equaliser, Clifton only partially saving East's shot after Parsons and Farquhar had had shots blocked.

A quick throw-in by Gordon enabled Nichols (R) to race away and only a very timely tackle by Harrington (M) saved a dangerous situation. Just before half time, Nichols (R) dribbled through only to shoot straight at Bowes from six yards range. A shot on the turn by Nichols (D) was only just off target.

Half time: Moseley United 0 Hen Lane Social 1

Hen Lane took up the attack on resuming and came close to increasing their lead when Preece hit an upright from a Nichols (D) pass. Keeping up the pressure, a long pass by Puffett put Nichols (D) away only for Bowes to dash out and block the shot.

Moseley drew level after fifty five minutes with a great goal. Parsons started the move with a crossfield pass to Hempshall and raced into position to neatly head in the return pass. When Pearce floated a free kick over the defence, Bevan raced in but failed to force the ball past Clifton. Hen Lane came back, and a move, which all forwards participated, ended when Bird shot wide from a good position. After seventy minutes Hen Lane regained the lead, Bird making an opening for Nichols (R) to shoot into the top corner of the net.

Full time: Moseley United 1 Hen Lane Social 2

07.02.1970   Moseley United seeking revenge for their President's Cup defeat, beat Hen Lane Social 2-1, Vallely scored both goals for the winners.

AC Godiva (formerly George Hudson FC) 1967/68 & 1968/69

17.10.1964   City Stars are now rivals!
George Curtis, skipper and centre half of Coventry City, has agreed to become President of Bradley United, the Coventry and District Sunday Junior League Club. George saw his side for the first time last weekend, when they won 4-1 over George Hudson FC, named after their President, the Sky Blues centre-forward. George Hudson missed last Sunday's derby as he was receiving treatment at Highfield Road. But he should be 'fit' to attend tomorrow's game, when the two teams meet in the return League match at Stoke Heath School pitch (11am). The two Georges are expected to run the lines.

19.12.1964   George Hudson FC started with seven players, and although three more came on later, reserve goalkeeper, Lissaman, was given a gruelling time.

07.09.1967   Close Athletic got off to their usual start, losing 3-1 to AC Godiva after the clubs had shared two goals in the first half.

28.09.1967   Division 3 Leaders, AC Godiva built up a good lead in the first half against Keresley Bell, but were fortunate as Keresley could manage to do everything but score in the second half and on this showing must surely soon move away from bottom place in the table. AC Godiva eventually won 5-2.

12.10.1967   AC Godiva, unbeaten leaders in Division 3, put up a commendable display against Division 1 Lime Tree Park, holding out until the fifty seventh minute, before conceding a goal. From this point on the experience of Lime Tree was noticeable and they eventually won 4-0, with Jim Garforth scoring all four.

19.10.1967   AC Godiva still retain the leadership in Division 3 but lost their unbeaten record to Colwyn Villa in an end-to-end game. Colwyn won 4-2.

09.11.1967   In Division 3, the match between Phoenix Royal and AC Godiva was anyone's right up until the final whistle. In a good first half Godiva took the lead, but shortly before half time Phoenix were awarded a penalty and equalised. In the second half Phoenix went into a 2-1 lead only for Godiva to level matters shortly after. Everything pointed to the teams sharing the points until shortly before the end when a second penalty for Phoenix, coverted by Starkey, gave them the points.

16.11.1967   AC Godiva remain leaders of Division 3, and two points from their meeting with Courtiers kept their promotion hopes alive. Godiva led 2-0 at half time. Ray Munday completed his hat-trick after the interval. Courtiers scored a consolation goal before Godiva netted their third.

30.11.1967   The match between the two leading clubs in Division 3 proved a real thriller, and going into extra time before Colwyn Villa eventually beat AC Godiva 2-1. Villa opened the scoring after fifteen minutes when Chris Bevan scored. Munday equalised for Godiva just before half time. Hughie Mitchell scored the winner in the second period of extra time. (Evening Telegraph Sunday Cup – 2nd Round)

04.01.1968   Division 3 was reduced to three matches and AC Godiva maintained their bid for promotion. Godiva, entertaining ten men Rugby Medina played some good football, considering the conditions, and although they only led 2-0 at half time the result was never in any doubt. Medina weakened after the interval and Godiva added five more goals.

07.03.1968 A goal in each half gave Railwaymens the points over AC Godiva, but the result was in doubt right until the final whistle.

21.03.1968 Division 1 side Poplar Athletic settled down early against AC Godiva and scored four in the first half. The second half proved more evenly matched with each side scoring twice. (Transport Shield – Senior Section)

04.04.1968 Colwyn Villa completed the double over AC Godiva and need only one point from their final fixture to win the Division title.

09.11.1968 A Lever threesome enabled AC Godiva to beat Parkstone B 5-2

21.12.1968 AC Godiva crushed Courtiers 10-1.

08.02.1969 Machin Athletic aided by four goals from Phil Lane, beat AC Godiva 7-0

29.03.1969 Railwaymens Club slipped in their bid to gain Division 1 football, being held to a goalless draw by AC Godiva.

05.04.1969 Shock result of the day was in the Senior League Division 2 where AC Godiva ended the unbeaten record of title chasing Youell Athletic, winning 1-0.

Parkstone WMC 1969/70 & 1970/71

20-09-69 Parkstone 'A' recorded one of their best performances when they easily beat Golden Cross Social 9-2 with G Dobbs scoring three.

11-10-69   Parkstone 'A', who have always figured among the also-rans in the Senior League, are making quite an impression and are unbeaten to date. They were the better side against Sporting Club New Star and deservedly won 5-1.

11-01-69   Spartak showed their best form against Parkstone'B', with Steve Riley netting three. Spartak coasted to a comfortable 8-1 win

18-10-69   Senior League Division 1 leaders Parkstone 'A' consolidated their lofty position with a 4-1 success over Awson Sports.

25-10-69   Parkstone 'B' beat Dunchurch by the odd goal in nine, Fletcher netting three for the visitors.

15-11-69   Big surprise in Division 2 of the Senior League was the 8-0 drubbing of GEC Electronics by Parkstone 'B', Graham Fletcher netting four.

22-11-69   Graham Fletcher grabbed four as leaders Parkstone 'A' marched on with a 10-1 trouncing of A C Godiva.

05-12-69   In the Senior League First Division leaders Parkstone 'A' struggled hard for their 1-0 victory against Colwyn Villa. Dave Price the Villa goalkeeper saved a penalty.

13-12-69   Division 2 title chasers Shakespeare United dropped a point when held 1-1 by Parkstone 'B'.

24-01-70   Other men on target in this division were Graham Fletcher (Parkstone 'B') who netted four in the 6-0 defeat of Coventry Climax.

31-01-70   Parkstone 'A' strengthened their lead with a fine 3-0 win over previously unbeaten Lenton's Lane.

07-02-70   Also through are Arley WMC 3-0 winners against Parkstone 'A'

28-02-70   In Division 1 of the Senior League, Parkstone 'B' dropped a valuable point against Wheel Wanderers.

07-03-70   Parkstone 'A' and Dolphin, setting the pace at the top of Division 1 of the Senior League, had convincing 5-0 and 6-0 successes over Wheel Wanderers and Radford Road United respectively. Both faced teams short of men.

28-03-70   Parkstone 'A' surrendered their unbeaten tag in the first division of the Senior League when beaten 4-3 by Dolphin Athletic.

25-04-70   Parkstone 'A' crushed A C Godiva 8-0

16-05-70   Dolphin clinched the Senior League Division 1 title when they beat ace rivals Parkstone 'A' 6-1. Parkstone, whose only other defeat was by Dolphin when the teams met at Longford Park, finish runners-up. All the goals came in the second half Parkstone losing their best chance when missing a penalty with Dolphin winning 3-1.

19-09-70   Buncranna Hearts, runaway winners of the Third Division last season, beat Parkstone 'B' 4-0.

03-10-70   In the Second Division GEC Electronics came to the end of their winning run when they were beaten 4-3 by Parkstone 'B'

24-10-70   Stoke Ex-Service commanded the first half of their President's Cup tie against Parkstone 'A' and deservedly led 2-0 at half-time. After the interval Parkstone pulled back a goal and squandered chances that would have given them the tie.

24-10-70   Parkstone 'B' had a field day in their Division 2 match against Greyfriars winning 7-1 with Graham Fletcher scoring three.

31-10-70   Parkstone 'B' did not show their league form when they played Fourth Division side Hearts United who won 3-2

14-11-70   Sporting Club Allesley Reserves suffered their first defeat when losing to Parkstone 'B'. The Club led 3-1 at one stage, but a second half hat-trick by Graham Fletcher clinched a valuable success for Parkstone.

28-11-70   In the Coventry and District League's Evening Telegraph Cup tie between Parkstone 'A' and Tile Hill Social the underdogs came out on top. After sharing two first half goals Parkstone got a 70th minute winner.

28-11-70   Parkstone 'B' are making a strong bid for honours and their 3-2 victory (after being behind at half time) over Ernesford Grange was well deserved.

12-12-70   Dolphin Athletic received a setback in the Premier League Second Division when they lost by a single first half goal to Parkstone 'A', the team they pipped for promotion from the Senior League last season.

12-12-70   Graham Fletcher had a great day for Parkstone 'B', scoring five and having one disallowed when helping his team to a 7-1 win against Greyfriars.

09-01-71   Parkstone 'B' well out in front in the Second Division, improved their goal average when they trounced Coventry Climax 11-0 with Graham Fletcher netting five goals.

16-01-71   Parkstone 'B', already assured of promotion from the Second Division, outclassed close rivals Buncranna Hearts 7-0. Hero for Parkstone was centre-forward Graham Fletcher, who scored six goals to take his tally for the season to 40.

06-02-71   In a CIU Cup game Parkstone Working Men's Club were too experienced for Stanton and soon built up a four goal lead. They were then content to sit back but ran out worthy 6-1 winners.

13-02-71   After giving Albany Social a three goal start in a second Division match, Parkstone 'A' dominated play during the second half, but could manage only to pull back two goals.

13-02-71   There was little to choose between GEC Electronics and Parkstone 'B' in the first half, but after the interval goals came to both sides, Parkstone winning 8-4 with Graham Fletcher scoring five.

20-02-71   Spartak were the only surprise winners in the quarter-finals beating Senior Division 2 pace-setters Parkstone 'B' 2-1 after scoring twice in the first period. Parkstone netted four times in the second period, but their efforts were disallowed three times for infringements.

27-02-71   Parkstone 'A', who have figured among the also-rans for some time, brought off the shock win of the round when the trounced Division 1 side Four Provinces 6-1 with Kevin Hill scoring a hat-trick.

06-03-71   After a goal-less first half Coventry Climax looked like salvaging a point against Parkstone 'A', but the Parkstone side hit form after the interval and netted five times.

06-03-71   Parkstone 'B' stretched their lead in Division 2 and in their last six matches have to meet the teams immediately below them in the table. Parkstone and Veterans shared two first half goals, but the Club had the better of the exchanges after the interval to win 5-2.

13-03-71   Dunchurch completed the Division 2 programme with a 4-2 victory against Parkstone 'A', but must wait several weeks to find if they will be champions or runners-up.

20-03-71   Albany Social put up a commendable performance in the second half of their match against Parkstone 'A'. Albany, trailing 3-0 at half-time came back and were unfortunate not to at least share the points, losing by the odd goal in seven.

20-03-71   Parkstone 'B' were lucky in their top of the table clash in the Second Division with Sporting Club Allesley, who played much better football but had to be content with sharing six goals.

27-03-71   Parkstone 'B' were on top throughout against Ernesford Grange, scoring at regular intervals to win 7-2 with Graham Fletcher netting five to bring his total to 55 for this season.

03-04-71   The Senior League Second Division has been thrown open again with the defeat of leaders Parkstone 'B', who looked to be romping away with the title. They failed to capitalise on chances and went under 0-2 to Pegasus.

10-04-71   In the Evening Telegraph Cup Poplar Athletic got through 3-1 against Parkstone 'A'

24-04-71   Stoke Ex-Service took a step nearer the Premier League Division 2 Title when they beat Parkstone 'A' 3-0.

01-05-71   Parkstone 'B' finished their Second Division Senior League matches with a flourish when they beat Veterans'65 6-0, but must await the final results of Buncranna Hearts before they know whether they are champions or runners-up.

08-05-71   The Senior League Division 2 title race has reached a very interesting situation. Parkstone 'B' and Buncranna Hearts both have one match to play and are level on points with very close goal averages

15-05-71   "Same goal average – so title shared"
Two clubs have shared the championship of the Coventry and District Senior League Division 2 and officials believe it is a unique situation. The clubs Parkstone 'B' and Buncranna Hearts both finished the season with 38 point from 22 games and identical goal averages, Buncranna scored 105 goals and conceded 42 and Parkstone's figures were 110 for and 44 against. Both sides had an average of 2.5.

Yet before each side played the last match, the odds against a championship tie were astronomical. The only way such a result could have happened was for Buncranna to win 5-4 and Parkstone to win 6-1, and that is just what happened!

Buncranna playing Sporting Club Allesley led 3-1 at one stage but found themselves level at 4-4 and only a late goal gave them the points. Parkstone completed their programme against Barras Green.

The two clubs will share the trophy instead of a play-off for the championship.

Avondale FC 1970/71 to 1972/73

31.10.1970   Doubleday, Section 'A' leaders, were 3-0 down to Avondale, but fought back to earn a 4-4 draw.

14.11.1970   Avondale moved to the top of Section 'A' following their 9-3 win over Hertford.

21.11.1970   In the League Invitation Cup, Avondale just deserved their 2-1 win over Coombe Social.

19.12.1970   Goals from Chadwick (2) and Sorrell gave Lanchester a 3-1 victory over Section 'A' leaders Avondale in the League Invitation Cup.

09.01.1971   Avondale kept their unbeaten record intact beating Homefire 3-0

23.01.1971   Section 'A' leaders Avondale suffered a shock 1-3 defeat by Keresdon Park

20.02.1971   An intriguing position is developing in Section 'A' with Avondale steadily gaining points and their nearest rivals losing form.

01.05.1971   Doubleday won their vital District League clash with Avondale to win the Section 'A' championship. They led 3-0 in the first half through Bingen (2) and Boston, but missed a penalty. Doubleday weathered the second half pressure and are the only unbeaten team in the league.

11.09.1971   Avondale were flattered by their win over Foleshill Athletic. They were leading by only one goal with ten minutes to go, and then grabbed another three in as many minutes.

18.09.1971   Doubleday shot to the top of Division 2 after beating Avondale 2-0 through goals by Whitehouse and Bingham

25.09.1971   After Osmond gave Avondale the lead against Motor Panels many scoring chances went begging and it wasn't until Smith equalised that Osmond was sparked into getting the winner.

02.10.1971   Avondale kept up the pressure on the leaders and took both points and a 2-0 win over Indian New Star – Osmond and Bird getting the goals.

09.10.1971   Goals by Colley (penalty) and Small gave Avondale a 2-1 win over Potters Green in the CET Junior Cup.

16.10.1971   Derek Hempshall, the Avondale secretary, played a major part in his club's 2-1 victory over his former club. Moseley led through a Shuttleworth own goal, but Osmond hit back for Avondale. Then Small grabbed the winner ten minutes from time after good work from Osmond.

23.10.1971   An excellent display by goalkeeper Tony Brown, earned Avondale two points against Coombe Social, and kept them in touch with the leaders. The goals came from Hempshall and Osmond.

30.10.1971   Avondale shared two goals with Meadway Reserves, Symonds scored for Meadway with Staff replying.

06.11.1971   Unluckiest team in the Boyd Carpenter Cup were Avondale. Two of their players - Bird and Colley - had to receive treatment after colliding, and the team went on to lose 2-1.

13.11.1971   Presidents Cup 1st Round.
                     Avondale v Coachmakers
A long throw by Cook went straight across the homesters' goal, but there was no-one there to take advantage of it. Helped by the wind, the visitors were giving Brown plenty to do, one long shot from Bolstridge hitting the crossbar and rebounding into play. At the other end Osmond brilliantly dribbled through the Coachmakers ' defence and then shot weakly into Morley's hands.
   In another combined move by the Avondale forwards Small went through and gave Morley no chance with his shot. A bad mistake by the

visitors defence allowed Adams to run through and increase Avondale's lead, but it was then reduced by Hughes.
Half time: Avondale 2 Coachmakers 1
Full time: Avondale2 Coachmakers 1

04.12.1971   Indian Commonwealth lost 2-0 to Avondale and the difference the defeat made in goal average put Doubleday back on top. Adams and Small hit the Avondale goals.

11.12.1971   Avondale hit back with goals from Small (3) and Osmond (2) to win 5-1 against Motor Panels after trailing.

11.12.1971   Presidents Cup 3rd Round
Avondale v Whoberley Wanderers
With the wind in their favour, Whoberley had the advantage. but Avondale keeping the ball close advanced and were awarded a free-kick, from which Bird shot wide. From a long goal kick by Corrigan, McDonagh raced away, but Brown came out to save his first shot and smothered the second.
  Small made a break down the wing, his centre was misjudged by Corrigan and Bird turned the ball past the post for Avondale. Whoberley equalised soon afterwards when McDonagh headed in from a corner.
Half time: Avondale 1 Whoberley 1
Full time: Avondale 1 Whoberley 2

08.01.1972   Avondale moved into third position with a 3-1 victory over Sherwyn, who took the lead through a penalty. Avondale scorers were Osmond (2) and Adams.

15.01.1972   Goals from corners by Hancox and Small gave Avondale a 2-1 win against Sherwyn Athletic.

05.02.1972   Avondale challenging for the leadership of Division 2, were lucky to earn both points by beating Meadway Reserves 5-4 after trailing 1-4

19.02.1972   Avondale went down to a surprise 3-5 defeat by Stoneleigh in a Division 2 match. John Smart the Stoneleigh goalkeeper, got his name on the scoresheet with an amazing goal. His clearance was mis-judged by Brown in the Avondale goal and the ball went directly into the net.

26.02.1972   Avondale, forced to make changes through injuries, went into an early two goal lead through Westgarth and Hempshall against Rayon. Then Rayon struck back with three quick goals for Cramp, Fenlon and Testot, but just before the interval Avondale got back on terms through Westgarth and there was no further scoring.

29.04.1972   Avondale slipped out of the race for the Division 2 title with defeats by Coombe and Foleshill.

30.09.1972   Defensive errors were responsible for the goals in the Keresdon – Avondale game and a tragic slip in the closing stages gave Avondale victory.

07.10.1971   Avondale failed to take a commanding lead at the top of the table when they slipped against Indian New Star.

21.10.1972   Meriden Rovers scored a goal in each half to beat out-of-form Avondale

28.10.1972   Avondale, leaders in Division 2, were trailing 1-4 at Foleshill and the hit back to force a draw in an exciting last ten minutes.

18.11.1972   Avondale returned to winning form with a 5-1 victory over Moseley United and had two other goals disallowed.

09.01.1973   Two Bob Colley penalties helped Avondale to a 3-1 win over Lyric

20.01.1973   New Star, Rayon and Avondale are now level at the top of the table on 21 points. Avondale moved to the top with an 8-0 win over Lyric with Small grabbing a hat-trick.

03.02.1973   Avondale, in second place in Division 2, earned themselves a 'four pointer' when they beat Rayon 4-0

10.02.1973   Avondale stay in top place in Division 2. Tommy Small grabbed a hat-trick in the 4-2 win over New Star.

17.02.1973   Small took his tally to 25 goals for the season when he scored both goals for Avondale in their 2-1 victory over Foleshill Athletic.

03.03.1973   Five goals in twenty minutes from Small (2), Hempshall, Staff and Sanders gave Avondale victory over 10 men Stoneleigh.

10.03.1973   Avondale kept top place in Division 2 with a 5-2 win over Coombe Social in which sharp-shooting winger Small scored four goals.

07.04.1973   Avondale are certain of promotion from Division 2 following their 2-0 victory over Meadway Reserves, but Rayon, three points behind with three games in hand, could pip them for the title.

Barras Green Rangers 1972/73
Coventry and District (Sunday) League Senior Divison 5

16-11-72   Barry Olden went nap against Stoneleigh, helping Barras Green Rangers win 9-0

21-10-72   Mason United went into extra time for the second week running against Barras Green Rangers. After 90 minutes the teams were level at 1-1 but Mason managed their ticket through to round two with a goal during extra time.

27-01-73   In a Division 5 match Barras Green Rangers' outside hopes of finishing with a chance of honours took a tumble when they went down by a single second half goal to AC XI.

03-02-73   Barras Green Rangers had a field day against Unbrako when they scored ten times against Unbrako without reply with J Foley scoring eight.

24-02-73   D Buckingham netted four times for Barras Green Rangers, helping his side win 8-3 against White Bear, for whom J McLellan scored a hat-trick.

Barras Green WMC 1973/74
Coventry and Central Warwickshire (Sunday) League Senior Division 2

22-09-73   A L Dunn's again lost by a narrow margin, Barras WMC edging home 4-2. Glynn, Johnson, Best and Smith scored for Barras with Twigger and Munro netting for Dunns.

13-10-73   Bubbenhall had no intention of playing Goliath to Barras Green's David and scored four times in the first ten minutes and added two more before the interval. Each side netted three times in the second half. Seventeen year old Roger Bennett, the discovery of the season, followed his hat-trick of last week with three more goals and also made two more. Other scorers were Gormley (2), Heathcote and Slevin, while Halcrow, Rust and Foley replied for Barras Green.

20-10-73   Barras Green and Builders kept up the pursuit of the leaders, scoring six each against Corinthians and Courthouse.

27-10-73   Barras Green won their important Division 2 clash against Standard Bearers and now head the table. Barras won 6-2 with Rust, Foley and Healey all scoring two. Wykes and Rouse scored for Bearers who were handicapped by the loss of a player through injury.

08-12-73   A surprise looked possible when Midland Rangers led Barras WMC in Division 2 thanks to a superb goal from Hillyer. Barras, with a 100 per cent record, came back to win narrowly with goals from Johns and Buckingham.

22-12-73   Barras WMC scraped home by the odd goal in seven against Builders Club in Division 2, and are now the only club left with a 100 per cent record.

05-01-74   Barras Green dropped their first point in Division 2 to Courthouse, who twice came from a goal down. Hill and Buckingham scored for Barras, Richardson and D Miles for Courthouse.

12-01-74   The top teams, Barras WMC and Standard Bearer also fought out a draw this being a league game, following their recent 3-3 cup clash. Buckingham gave Barras the lead, but some poor finishing, together with good saves from O'Sullivan prevented them from increasing the margin, and Cox equalised.

19-01-74   Barras WMC emphasised their superiority in Division 2, hammering third placed Newtown Athletic 9-1. Glynn (2), Halcrow (2), Hill, Buckingham, Johnson and Johns were the scorers, with a consolation effort coming from Reid.

26-01-74   Barras WMC took another step toward the Division 2 title. Coombe Social led briefly through a Portlock goal, but the Barras rattled up seven, Foley hitting a hat-trick and Buckingham two.

16-02-74   Second Division leaders Barras WMC must have felt pretty sick after hammering eight goals in 65 minutes past Corinthians, only for further heavy rain to force an abandonment. Buckingham (3), Brick, John, Foley, Halcrow and Farquharson all netted, but might just as well stayed in bed!

02-03-74   Barras WMC reached the final of the C T Cooke Cup in convincing style, hammering Builders Club 7-2. Builders held the score to 2-2 at half time before being overwhelmed. Buckingham (3) and Halcrow (2) led the scoring.

09-03-74   The biggest surprise of the day was the defeat of Barras WMC by Courthouse. D Miles (2) and Taylor netted for Courthouse, Barrras replying through Halcrow and Johnson.

20-04-74   Barras WMC won the Second Division of the Senior League in amazing style, slaughtering poor Corinthians 19-1. Bobby Halcrow scored seven, Buckingham five and Foley four. To their credit Corinthians kept trying to the final whistle.

11-05-74   Barras WMC and Newtown Athletic provided splendid entertainment in the Tom Cooke Cup final, Barras squeezing home 4-3. Barras, receiving tremendous encouragement for a large band of supporters, took the lead through Bobby Halcrow only for Reid to equalise immediately. Ron Chapman gave Newtown the lead, but Foley made the scores level on the stroke of half-time. Each side scored again soon after the interval, with Buckingham making the most of a Newtown mistake and Reid hitting his second of the day in reply, The game was won with a brilliant Halcrow goal, but it was a desperately close finish. Barras thus completed a Cup and League double.

Barras Green Rangers 1974/75
Coventry and District (Saturday) League Section 'B'

07-09-74   Barras Green playing their first game in the league, ran riot against Bubbenhall Reserves scoring ten goals without reply.

05-10-74   In Section 'B', Buckingham scored seven of Barras Green's goals in their 11-1 win against New Hillfields, but Barras were brought down to earth when the young Edgewick team defeated them 2-1 thanks to a last minute penalty by Hastings. Earlier Barras had missed a twice-taken spot kick.

19-10-74   Barras Rangers defeated Keresdon Reserves by 4-1 with goals from Farquharson (2), Mulhearn and O'Connor. The game was marred by David Buckingham of Barras breaking a leg.

16-11-74   GNP Reserves and Barras Green fought out a 2-2 draw after extra-time.

21-12-74   Barras Green kept up their title challenge with a 7-0 win against Tandee Reserves, thanks to four goals from Foley and further goals from Mulhearn (2) and Rooney.

18-01-75   Barras Green are keeping hard on the heels of Edgewick. They kept up their impressive form by defeating Cheylesmore by 5-0. K Mulhearn (2), G Farquharson, T Toal and J Foley netted for Barras. The battle for a Section 'B' now looks to be between Edgewick and Barras and this could be decided in a few weeks time when the meet.

08-02-75   Clifton moved into their first Cup final since 1968 when they beat Kingfield 3-1 in the semi-finals of the Coventry Evening Telegraph Minor Cup. The other semi-final between Barras Green

Rangers and Minster Rangers was postponed because of a waterlogged pitch and will be played next Saturday.

23-02-75 Barras Green in their first season in Saturday football since 1966, moved into the final of the Telegraph Minor Cup, when they overcame Minster Rangers to win 4-3 after extra-time. Referee John Jackson said, "This was a superb example of how football should be played. Both teams were a credit to the competition and it was unfortunate that one side had to lose. A tribute to the standard of football played by Minster Rangers came from a Barras official, who said that although they were delighted to have reached the final the better side on the day lost. Minster led at half-time 1-0, but at the end the score was 2-2. Goals for Minster were scored by Raj Mattu, Sunil Nahar and Amarjit Singh while Barras's goals came from T Foley, K Foley, Toal and Rooney.

08-03-75 Edgewick United made sure of the Section 'B' title in their first season when beating Brookstray by a single goal. Roger Reeves and John Kelly netted for Cheylesmore in the defeat of Barras.

29-04-75 "Farquharson hit winner" Barras Green Rangers are the last holders of the Coventry Evening Telegraph Minor Cup. They won the final by beating Clifton 2-1 after extra-time at Courtaulds Ground last night. The Barras hero was Grant Farquharson, who shot home the winning goal to end a gallant fight by Clifton, who had taken the lead in the first half, but Barras applied pressure after half-time and equalised through Jack Foley.

03-05-75 Barras Green lifted the Section 'B' Supplementary Cup by defeating New Hillfields 3-0.

Barras Green WMC 1974/75
Coventry and Central Warwickshire (Sunday) League Division 1

07-09-74   The first half of the Barras - Newtown match was reminiscent of last season's thrilling Tom Cooke Cup final, but Newtown faded badly after the break. Bobby Halcrow knocked in four of the eight Barras goals.

14-09-74   Barras had little difficulty beating Minster 9-2

12-10-74   Senior League leaders lost their position on a disastrous match against Barras. Halcrow (3), Buckingham (2) and Foley (2) shared the Barras goals.

19-10-74   Barras Green caused one of the big shocks knocking out Premier 2 leaders Padmore Rovers. Bobby Halcrow gave Barras the lead before a Steve Brown hat-trick put Padmore on top at the interval. Then Barras scored three times, Padmore equalised before an own goal decided an excellent attacking game.

02-11-74   Social Services gave Barras Green a good run for their money in Senior Division 1 but defensive slips helped Barras to a 2-1 victory. Bobby Halcrow and Kevin Foley were the Barras marksmen, Crawley replying.

16-11-74   Celtic Travellers were unlucky with injuries and lost their unbeaten record to Barras Green in an F H Ogg Cup tie.It was a cracking game and Barras took their chances to win 4-2.

23-11-74   All four Senior Division 1 games went with the form book. The most emphatic was Barras's nine-goal success against a gallant Corinthians Whitmore side. Bobby Halcrow led the spree with five goals.

30-11-74   Barras had a scare when Martin Newman and John Crawley scored early goals for Social Services, but came back to lead by the interval, and score again in the second half. (Halcrow (2), Foley and Masters (pen) were their marksmen.

01-01-75   Barras Green were not in the mood for charity against Mowog in the Senior Division 1, scoring seven times in each half. Jack Foley led the scoring with four, Kevin Foley and Grant Farquharson each netting three.

02-03-75   Mowog came close to upsetting Barras in the Senior Division 1, leading 2-0 at the break, Barras pulled level only to trail 3-2 before netting four late goals.

29-03-75   Barras Green reached the final of the F H Ogg Cup but were extended by lowly Corinthians Whitmore. Farquharson, Jack Foley and Kevin Foley took advantage of defensive slips to make sure of a Butts place.

05-04-75   "At Last 'Green' Lose A Game".
Barras Green's magnificent run of success came to an end in a routine Coventry and Central Warwicks League match with Minster Rangers. After a run of 16 successive wins which had taken them to the quarter final of the V L Edmonds Cup, the final of the F H Ogg Cup and second place in the Senior Division 1, Green crashed 3-1. Minster, an unpredictable side, led by the only goal at the interval, and netted twice in the second period. Barras's only reply was a penalty from full back Masters. Minster's marksmen were Amrik (2) and Binder.

19-04-75   Three wins in six days have given Barras a great chance of the Senior Division 1 title with a double over Celtic Travellers, the present leaders by a 3-0 margin on both occasions, and a 4-3 success against Bridge End Reserves in a Cup final rehearsal.

26-04-75   Barras, from the Senior League had most of the play against Premier League Glade, but defensive errors let them down. Glade, running out 4-1 winners.

24-05-75   The F H Ogg Cup for the Senior Division 1 sides went Barras Green, who had already won the league. Stuart Fisher gave Bridge End Reserves an early lead with a beautifully made goal, but Billy Masters soon equalised, and the game was decided when the Bridge End goalkeeper, under pressure, punched the ball into his own net.

Barras Green Rangers 1975/76
Coventry and District (Saturday) League Section 'A'

20-09-75   In section 'A' Barras Green showed the form which won them promotion when they defeated GEC Sports 4-1 with goals from G Farquharson, A Hill, D O'Connor and A Timms. K Reid netted for Sports.

27-09-75   Rooney, Foley and Mulhearn were on the mark for Barras in their 3-2 victory over Tile Hill in a Section 'A' Match. Rob Misstear and Ron Chapman replied.

11-10-75   "Lucky 13 For Barras Green". Highest score in the Coventry Evening Telegraph Junior Cup for several years went to Barras Green, who scored 13 against fellow District League team SNR. Green won the Minor Cup last season and won this time through Halcrow (5), Farquharson (4), Mulhearne (2), Leese and Foley.

18-10-75   Goals by Mulhearn (2) Halcrow, Farquharson, Foley and Rooney gave Barras Green a 6-0 victory over Phoenix.

22-11-75   Barras Green remained top of Section 'A' when they beat Cheylesmore 3-1 despite losing the goalkeeper early in the game.

Mulhearn (2) and Foley scored for Green after Kielly had given Cheylesmore the lead.

29-11-75   Leaders Barras hammered Self Change Gears 6-1 with Mulhearn hitting a hat-trick.

13-12-75   Section 'A' leaders Barras Green are still the only team with a 100 per cent record in the league, and they outclassed Phoenix A by 8-1. Foley led the scoring with a hat-trick and Glynn and O'Connor grabbed a couple each with Farquharson adding one.

20-12-75   Barras Green, one of the favourites in the Invitation Cup, beat Hall Green 6-0 through Mulhearn (2), Foley, Farquharson and O'Connor.

27-12-75   Barras Green, on top of Section 'A', pulled off a 3-2 away win over close rivals Edgewick United.

17-01-76   Barras Green, progressed into the semi-finals with an 8-1 mauling of Tandee Reserves, Foley scoring four goals.

31-01-76   Section 'A' leaders pressed on toward the title with a 3-0 away win at Hall Green, thanks to goals from P Glynn (2) and D Buckingham.

07-02-76   Leaders Barras Green still have their 100 per cent record after 14 games, but they had to work hard to pip Edgewick United by the odd goal in three, Billy Masters getting the two goals.

14-02-76   Section 'A' leaders Barras Green had no trouble accounting for lowly Whexford United. Foley and Buckingham each scored four in the 9-0 rout.

21-02-76   Barras Green, runaway leaders of Section 'A', thrashed Brookstray 7-0 through Mulhearn (2), T Foley, Farquharson, K Foley, Buckingham and J Foley.

28-02-76   Hopes by Barras, the Section 'A' leaders, of completing the season with a 100 per cent record were shattered when promotion hopefuls Tile Hill OB held them 1-1. The Old Boys led for most of the game with a goal for Sandy Reid, and it was only a late own gaol that enabled Barras to save a point.

27-03-76   Section 'A' leaders Barras Green had no trouble keeping their unbeaten record when they defeated Hen Lane Res 6-3 with Buckingham, Foley and Mulhearn grabbing two goals apiece. Crisp, Robson and McIntosh replied. Barras now need three points from their last four games to clinch the title.

27-03-76   Star Junior Match by Frank Thomas
Foleshill Athletic 3 Barras Green 0

Barras Green joined the District League last season and won promotion to section 'A' which they head at the present. They were also winners of the Telegraph Minor Cup. Foleshill Athletic, after a period in the Nuneaton Amateurs League, joined the District League last season and won promotion to Division 1. They occupy a mid-table position.
Barras Green: P John, M John, Halcrow, Dunne, T Foley, K Foley, Hill, P Glynn, J Foley, Buckingham, Mulhearn. Sub: M Glynn.
Foleshill Athletic: Preswick, Fellows, Tabberner, Rance, O'Shea, Anslow, Bratby, Calcott, Tipper, Griffiths, Hill. Sub: Squires.
Referee: Mr G Driver

Hill started his hat-trick for Foleshill two minutes after Fellows was carried off. With a strong wind behind them, Foleshill were soon on the attack and John came out to collect intended through passes, and then following a free-kick from Anslow, Griffiths header was scrambled away. Barras Green broke away only for Mulhearn to run offside and spoil a promising move. Foleshill went close to taking the lead when

Calcott's 25 yard free-kick beat the goalkeeper only to strike the angle of the crossbar and rebound to safety. Keeping up the pressure John could only push out a cross from Tipper, and Hall following up just failed to reach the loose ball. Barras again broke away through Mulhearn only for his centre to float over the goal area with no-one in position. Anslow combined with Calcott and only a timely intervention by M John prevented Calcott from getting clear.

After 20 minutes, Fellows was carried off injured and taken to hospital, and the substitute came on. Foleshill had a narrow escape when Buckingham headed past Prestwick but O'Shea was in position to kick off the goal line. After 22 minutes Foleshill went in front. Hill hitting home into the corner of the net, and in the next minute a lob from the same player bounced over the goalkeeper into the net. Play was mostly in the Barras Green half and John held a good header by Rance and then when Bratby was brought down just outside the penalty area Hill hit the free-kick home for his hat-trick. Barras fought back and Buckingham failed by inches to connect from J Foley's cross and O'Shea cleared with Mulhearn closing in and Prestwick held a free-kick from M John.

In another attack Prestwick raced to the edge of the penalty area to beat K Foley to a long ball. Foleshill replied and John snatched the ball from Griffith's head, and Anslow shot high over. At the other end J Foley was brought down when racing through and only for K Foley to hit the free-kick too high.

Half Time: Barras Green 0 Foleshill Athletic 3

Barras resumed on the attack and Mulhearn shot weakly straight at the goalkeeper form a good position, and Halcrow missed his kick when only six yards out. In another attack Preswick was quickly off his line to beat Mulhearn to a through pass and when Buckingham raced onto a free-kick his header flashed just high. Foleshill broke away and Griffiths fastened on to a through pass but John parried his fierce shot and Tipper hit the rebound back only for his shot to be diverted outside for a fruitless corner. Barras went close on two occasions Halcrow volleyed a first time effort inches wide and Buckingham was just off

target with a good header. Barras were putting on heavy pressure with mainly long range efforts which Preswick dealt with confidently.
Full time: Barras Green 0 Foleshill Athletic 3

17-04-76   Foley hit a hat-trick for Section 'A' champions Barras Green as they crushed Hertford United 5-1.

24-04-76   Section 'A' champions Barras Green went on a scoring spree against Self Change Gears when they won 8-1 to chalk up their 100 goals for the season. Halcrow (3) Mulhearn J Foley, K Foley and Riley were on the mark.

Barras Green WMC 1975/76
Coventry and Central Warwickshire (Sunday) League Premier Div'n 2

04-10-75   Rooney opened his account for his new club, Barras WMC, in fine style, scoring four in the heavy defeat of Brassworkers.

11-10-75   Barras Green had little trouble in progressing to the next round with a 5-2 victory over City Engineers.

25-10-75   John scored three for Barras Green, but they surprisingly dropped a Second Division point to plucky Jules Verne, who were twice behind but earned a 4-4 draw.

01-11-75   Jack Foley's three goals against Brassworkers kept Barras at the top of Division 2.

08-11-75   Barras Green had most of the play against Glade Reserves, but had moments of anxiety before running out 4-2 winners.

15-11-75   An O'Neill penalty was enough to give Celtic Travellers victory over keen rivals Barras Green.

29-11-75   Barras Green had surprising difficulty against Glade Reserves but a Bobby Halcrow hat-trick made sure of the points.

13-12-75   Kevin Mulhearn's hat-trick kept Barras Green well in contention in Division 2 sinking Bubbenhall Village 5-1.

17-01-76   Barras Green won the vital Second Division clash with Royal Oak, coming out on top 5-3 after conceding the first goal in a fine game.

07-02-76   Barras Green found it difficult to hit top form against nine-man Minster Rangers but were never in danger of surrendering a point, Bobby Halcrow and Grant Farquharson sharing four of the goals.

14-02-76   Barras Green took another step nearer the First Division, but Redburn Henley fully extended them, and the game was not safe until Lewis completed his hat-trick from the penalty spot three minutes from time.

21-02-76   In Division 2, Barras Green took themselves to within one point of a First Division place by beating 1925 Club.

28-02-75   Barras Green clinched the Second Division championship in great style, thrashing promotion hopefuls Jules Verne 8-1. Verne led through a Grant goal at the break, but had no answer to the second half finishing of the visitors, Dave Buckingham grabbing four and Grant Farquharson and Pete Glynn two apiece.

06-03-76   The race for promotion from Division 2 was made even hotter by the defeat of Barras Green, their first of the season in league games, by Celtic Travellers. Celtic ran up a three goal lead by the break, and Barras's rally was not enough to prevent a 5-2 loss, Cox and O'Neill scoring two each.

13-03-76   Royal Oak responded magnificently to their difficult task in the Second Division, virtually clinching promotion by beating champions Barras Green 4-3.

20-03-76   Second Division champions Barras Green finished their league season on a winning note, beating Redburn Henley by the only goal.

10-04-76   "Bold Barras lift Owen Cup"
Barras Green won the Coventry and Central Warwickshire Leagues' Tom Owen Cup when they beat Celtic Travellers 2-1 after extra-time in the final at the Butts Stadium. It took a goal by Dave Buckingham midway through the extra period to clinch a hard earned success for the Barras outfit. The Celtic Travellers defence was caught square after only 10 minutes when Bobby Halcrow picked up a long through ball to score past the advancing goalkeeper. An error by the Barras goalkeeper let in Bernard O'Neill for the equaliser after the break. Despite terrific pressure from both sides there was no scoring in normal time.

Apollo Rangers FC 1975/76 to 1977/78
Colliers FC 1978/79

20-09-75   Mowog played some attractive football with Dave Crossley scoring a well-taken hat-trick they beat Apollo Rangers 0-4

08-11-75   City Treasurers found the extra effort to win 3-2 in a keenly contested match against Apollo Rangers.

22-11-75   Coventry Evening Telegraph beat Apollo Rangers 2-0. Malcolm Palmer and Ken Widdows (penalty) netting the goals.

29-11-75   Apollo Rangers fought back in the second half against Walsgrave WMC to share six goals.

20-12-75   Sweeney Todd keep going strong at the top of Division 4 They kept their 100 percent record intact with a 2-0 victory against Apollo Rangers.

07-02-76   After a goalless first half Wyken Pippin move up into third spot with a 2-0 victory against Apollo Rangers.

16-10-76   Apollo Rangers slammed Pegasus 12-0 with Lol Anderson scoring four and Bobby Caves three.

23-10-76   Parkstone 'A' looked more like their old selves against Apollo Rangers scoring four goals without reply.

06-11-76   Godiva Rangers are still unbeaten in Division 4 but against Apollo Rangers it was touch and go before two goals direct from free kicks by S. Burdett gave Godiva a narrow 2-1 victory.

15-01-77   Painted lady and Apollo Rangers finished 4-4 and Apollo took the tie on penalties.

09-04-77   City Treasurers dropped a vital point when they were held 1-1 by Apollo Rangers.

30-04-77   Division 4 is still wide open, Godiva Rangers, who were favourites were beaten 3-0 by Apollo Rangers.

07-05-77   Potters Green beat Apollo Rangers from Division 4 by 2-0.

21-05-77   Coventry Evening Telegraph finished badly after looking at one stage likely candidates for honours. Apollo Rangers dominated throughout and were worthy 6-3 winners over the Press men.

12-11-77   Mowog keep up their challenge at the top of Division 4 but had a hard fight before beating Apollo Rangers 3-2.

03-12-77   Apollo Rangers were too strong for Coventry Evening Telegraph, winning 6-0.

01-04-78   Mike Malyon, playing his first full game since breaking a leg last October, grabbed two goals as Coventry Evening Telegraph fought a thrilling 3-3 draw with promotion chasing Apollo Rangers.

07-10-78   Colliers were in fine fettle against Woodlands, Eddy Robson scoring four and John Garner a hat-trick as they won 8-1.

21-10-78   Barry Machin scored four for Colliers as they overran Cov-Rad to take an easy 8-1 victory.

25-11-78   Chestnut Villa rose to the occasion in their match with Colliers and two goals in each half were enough to give their 4-2 win.

16-12-78   Colliers were the better side for the first twenty minutes against Barras Club but lost 4-2

20-01-79   City Treasurers and Colliers fought a goalless first half, but then the sparks flew as Colliers took their chances and emerged 5-2 winners.

07-04-79   The verdict between Colliers and Post Office Sports could have gone either way, Colliers winning by the odd goal in three.

Part 5 Results and Tables

The lists of results that follow have been obtained from archived microfilm records of the Coventry Evening Telegraph's Sports Edition, "The Pink", held at the History Centre of The Herbert Art Gallery and Museum. Fixtures were usually published in the normal editions toward the end of the week, so in theory, you knew which team was playing who, but it was subject to change. Some results and tables did not appear at all, and consequently there are some blank spaces in the lists.

There were various reasons for this, sometimes the Telegraph microfilmed the Leamington, Rugby or Nuneaton editions and the Coventry Leagues did not appear in those editions. The weather played a big part in the publishing of data, inasmuch that heavy rain, snow and ice led to delays in acquiring the results, as well as the postponement of fixtures. The build-up of fixtures meant that teams were still trying to complete their fixtures at the end of May. 'The Pink' would use their editorial precedent reporting of summer sports, such as Cricket, Tennis, Bowls and Speedway, and omitting results and final tables.

League tables were also affected; perhaps some fixtures were never completed when the issues of promotion and relegation had been confirmed. Missing results can sometimes be calculated even though the Opponents may not be known. The League tables are printed during the season, and with a bit of detective work it is possible to fill in some of the gaps in the tables. There are errors between the results summary and the 'final' league tables, Perfection is not guaranteed!

The cost of obtaining copies of all the information required to produce these lists is a staggering £400, but what you have to take into account is that the Reader/Printers used at the History Centre are in fact Antiques, and the cost of maintenance and replacement parts (if they are available) is astronomic.

It is fascinating reading through the pages of reports on grassroots football, and being able to recall, or maybe not, the events of the 1960's and 1970's, which in my opinion were the golden decades of the Twentieth Century.

Moseley United FC
Coventry and District (Saturday) Football League
Division 1 Results 1963/64

Opponents	Res	P	W	D	L	F	A	Pts
YCW	D3-3	1	0	1	0	3	3	1
Hastings Utd.	L0-9	2	0	1	1	3	12	1
St Lukes	L2-5	3	0	1	2	5	17	1
Cheylesmore	L0-2	4	0	1	3	5	19	1
Unbrako Res.	L1-4	5	0	1	4	6	23	1
Radford Utd.	L1-3	6	0	1	5	7	26	1
Fillongley	L0-3	7	0	1	6	7	29	1
Canley Social	L0-6	8	0	1	7	7	35	1
Tile Hill O.B.	L0-5	9	0	1	8	7	40	1
YCW	L0-8	10	0	1	9	7	48	1
Radford Utd.	L3-8	11	0	1	10	10	56	1
Cov. Pegasus	L1-2	12	0	1	11	11	58	1
Tile Hill O.B.	W2-1	13	1	1	11	13	59	3
Baginton B.L.	W3-2	14	2	1	11	16	61	5
Cheylesmore	L0-5	15	2	1	12	16	66	5
Hastings Utd.	L4-10	16	2	1	13	20	76	5
Canley FC	L3-4	17	2	1	14	23	80	5
St Lukes	W4-2	18	3	1	14	27	82	7
Fillongley	L0-12	19	3	1	15	27	94	7
Canley Social	L2-5	20	3	1	16	29	99	7
Canley FC	D1-1	21	3	2	16	30	100	8
Unbrako Res.	L0-5	22	3	2	17	30	105	8

Desperate times!

Moseley United Reserves
Coventry and District (Saturday) Football League
Junior Division Results 1963/64

Opponents	Res	P	W	D	L	F	A	Pts
Sherbourne Res.	L0-5	1	0	0	1	0	5	0
Coombe Social	L4-6	2	0	0	2	4	11	0
Baginton B.L.	D3-3	3	0	1	2	7	14	1
	L1-3	4	0	1	3	8	17	1
Allesley Park Res.	W6-4	5	1	1	3	14	21	3
Brassworkers	L0-5	6	1	1	4	14	26	3
	L	7	1	1	5			3
	L	8	1	1	6	19	36	3
Brinklow Res.	L1-7	9	1	1	7	20	43	3
Sherwyn Albion	D3-3	10	1	2	7	23	46	4
Brassworkers	L4-7	11	1	2	8	27	53	4
	L0-5	12	1	2	9	27	58	4
Sherbourne Res.	L1-4	13	1	2	10	28	62	4
Sherwyn Albion	L2-8	14	1	2	11	30	70	4
Brinklow Res.	W2-0	15	2	2	11	32	70	6
Whoberley Res	W2-1	16	3	2	11	34	71	8
		17	3	2	12	34	75	8
Coombe Social	L1-4	18	3	2	13	35	79	8
Avondale	W9-2	19	4	2	13	44	81	10
Veasey&Sharples	W4-3	20	5	2	13	48	84	12
Courtaulds App's	L1-2	21	5	2	14	49	86	12
Veasey&Sharples	L1-2	22	5	2	15	50	86	12
Electricity Res.	D1-1	23	5	3	15	51	87	13
Baginton B.L.	W3-0	24	6	3	15	54	87	15
	W	25	7	3	15			17
	W	26	8	3	15	61	90	19

Coventry and District (Saturday) Football League
Division 1 Table 1963/64

	P	W	D	L	F	A	Pts
Canley Social	21	19	2	0	97	20	40
Hastings Utd	20	16	0	4	117	30	32
Fillongley	22	14	1	7	97	58	29
Canley FC	19	13	2	4	76	37	28
St Lukes	21	12	2	7	67	46	26
Radford Utd	22	10	1	11	62	71	21
Baginton B.L.	21	8	3	10	54	71	19
Cheylesmore	22	7	1	14	50	93	15
YCW	20	6	1	13	49	72	13
Unbrako Res.	22	6	0	16	42	91	12
Tile Hill O.B.	22	5	1	16	42	82	11
Moseley Utd	**22**	**3**	**2**	**17**	**30**	**105**	**8**

Junior Division Table 1963/64

Brassworkers	26	22	1	3	138	39	45
Cov Pegasus Res.	26	19	2	5	111	48	30
Sherbourne Res	26	18	2	6	103	50	38
Coombe Social	25	15	2	8	113	62	32
Courtaulds Apps	26	13	5	8	78	61	31
Sherwyn Albion	25	13	4	8	87	60	30
Electricity Res	25	9	8	8	67	72	26
Baginton B.L. Res	24	11	2	11	73	78	24
Veasey & Sharples	26	8	5	13	70	96	21
Allesley Park Res	25	8	5	12	76	85	21
Moseley Utd Res	**26**	**8**	**3**	**15**	**61**	**90**	**19**
Whoberley Res	25	7	1	17	57	92	15
Avondale	26	4	2	20	42	155	10
Brinklow Res	26	2	0	23	40	128	4

Moseley United FC
Coventry and District (Saturday) Football League
Division 2 Results 1964/65

Opponents	Res	P	W	D	L	F	A	Pts
Allesley Park	W8-0	1	1	0	0	8	0	2
	W3-2	2	2	0	0	11	2	4
Cov Pegasus Res.	W2-0	3	3	0	0	13	2	64
	W	4	4	0	0			8
	W	5	5	0	0	25	4	10
	L2-4	6	5	0	1	27	8	10
Unicorn Celtic	W4-2	7	6	0	1	31	10	12
	W	8	7	0	1			14
Pinley C.C.	W	9	8	0	1	42	14	16
Allesley Park	W4-0	10	9	0	1	46	14	18
Ryton United	W4-3	11	10	0	1	50	17	20
St Lukes Res.	W8-3	12	11	0	1	58	20	22
Sherbourne O.B.	W8-0	13	12	0	1	66	20	24
St Lukes Res.	W2-0	14	13	0	1	68	20	26
Howitzers	W5-2	15	14	0	1	73	22	28
Meriden Rovers	D2-2	16	14	1	1	75	24	29
Howitzers	L2-4	17	14	1	2	77	28	29
Cov Pegasus Res.	W6-0	18	15	1	2	83	28	31
Meriden Rovers	L1-2	19	15	1	3	84	30	31
Beechwood Res.	W2-1	20	15	1	3	86	31	33
Pinley C.C.	W4-2	21	17	1	3	90	33	35
Unicorn Celtic	D4-4	22	17	2	3	94	37	36

Moseley United Reserves
Coventry and District (Saturday) Football League
Junior Division Results 1964/65

Opponents	Res	P	W	D	L	F	A	Pts
Allesley Park Res	W4-0	1	1	0	0	4	0	2
Allesley Park Res	W6-2	2	2	0	0	10	2	4
Trinity United	W3-2	3	3	0	0	13	4	6
	L	4	3	0	1			6
	L	5	3	0	2			6
	L	6	3	0	3	17	17	6
Sherbourne Res	W3-2	7	4	0	3	20	19	8
Tile Hill OB Res	L0-1	8	4	0	4	20	20	8
	D	9	4	1	4			9
	D	10	4	2	4			10
	L	11	4	2	5	23	31	10
Veasey&Sharples	W8-2	12	5	2	5	31	33	12
Veasey&Sharples	W3-1	13	6	2	5	34	34	14
	W	14	7	2	5			16
	L	15	7	2	6	39	40	16
Tile Hill OB Res	W4-0	16	8	2	6	43	40	18
Avondale	D1-1	17	8	3	6	44	41	19
Whoberley Res	W4-2	18	9	3	6	48	43	21
Sherwyn Alb Res	W9-1	19	10	3	6	57	44	23
Queen Margarets	L2-7	20	10	3	7	59	51	23

Coventry and District (Saturday) Football League
Division 2 Table 1964/65

	P	W	D	L	F	A	Pts
Moseley United	**22**	**17**	**2**	**3**	**94**	**37**	**36**
Meriden Rovers	22	15	4	3	69	35	34
Howitzers O.C.	22	16	0	6	89	48	29
Pinley CC	22	14	1	7	76	39	28
Kenilworth B L	22	13	1	8	73	60	26
Unicorn Celtic	22	10	5	7	50	33	21
Beechwood Res	22	9	5	8	58	54	19
Sherbourne O B	22	8	1	13	66	89	15
St Lukes Res.	22	7	2	13	46	54	13
Ryton United	22	6	0	15	42	60	12
Cov Pegasus Res	22	3	1	18	32	96	11
Allesley Park	22	3	0	19	33	114	8

Junior Division Table 1964/65

	P	W	D	L	F	A	Pts
Meadway Rvs Res	20	18	1	1	98	36	37
Queen Margarets	20	17	1	2	116	30	35
Avondale	20	11	1	8	74	44	23
Moseley Utd Res	**20**	**10**	**3**	**7**	**59**	**51**	**23**
Veasey & Sharples	20	10	1	9	71	53	21
Sherbourne Res	20	9	1	10	54	64	19
Tile Hill OB Res	20	9	0	11	39	62	18/
Whoberley W Res	20	5	4	11	43	68	14
Sherwyn Alb. Res	20	6	1	13	40	88	13
Allesley Park Res	20	3	4	13	37	83	10
Trinity United	20	4	1	15	51	109	9

Moseley United FC
Coventry and District (Saturday) Football League
Division 1 Results 1965/66

Opponents	Res	P	W	D	L	F	A	Pts
Meriden Rovers	D3-3	1	0	1	0	3	3	1
Tile Hill O.B.	W2-0	2	1	1	0	5	3	3
Beechwood	W4-1	3	2	1	0	9	4	5
Beechwood	W3-1	4	3	1	0	12	5	7
Balsall /Berkswell	W9-2	5	4	1	0	21	7	9
Howitzers	L0-3	6	4	1	1	21	10	9
St Lukes	L0-2	7	4	1	2	21	12	9
Fillongley	L0-1	8	4	1	3	21	13	9
Unicorn Celtic	L4-5	9	4	1	4	25	18	9
Howitzers	W6-4	10	5	1	4	31	22	11
Meadway Rvrs.	L3-5	11	5	1	5	34	27	11
Stoke Aldermoor	D0-0	12	5	2	5	34	27	12
Fillongley	L2-4	13	5	2	6	36	31	12
Unicorn Celtic	L0-1	14	5	2	7	36	35	12
Folly Lane	W3-1	15	6	2	7	39	36	14
Balsall/Berkswell	W10-2	16	7	2	7	49	38	16
Stoke Aldermoor	L1-6	17	7	2	8	50	44	16
Meriden Rovers	D3-3	18	7	3	8	53	47	17
Folly Lane	L	19	7	3	9			17
St Lukes	L	20	7	3	10	55	51	17
Tile Hill O.B	D1-1	21	7	4	10	56	52	18
Meadway Rvrs.	W2-0	22	8	4	10	58	52	20

Moseley United Reserves
Coventry and District (Saturday) Football League
Section 'A' Results 1965/66

Opponents	Res	P	W	D	L	F	A	Pts
Christ Church	W2-1	1	1	0	0	2	1	2
Jubilee Athletic	W3-1	2	2	0	0	5	2	4
Tile Hill OB Res	L1-2	3	2	0	1	6	4	4
Sherwyn Ath Res	W3-2	4	3	0	1	9	6	6
Whexford	L0-2	5	3	0	2	9	6	6
Veterans	W5-1	6	4	0	2	14	7	8
Sherbourne Res	D2-2	7	4	1	2	16	9	9
Brassworkers R	W9-0	8	5	1	2	25	9	11
Whoberley Res	W4-0	9	6	1	2	29	9	13
Baginton B L	D2-2	10	6	2	2	31	11	14
Avondale	L1-5	11	6	2	3	32	16	14
Whoberley Res	W1-0	12	7	2	3	33	16	16
Jubilee Athletic	W5-4	13	8	2	3	38	20	18
Tile Hill OB Res	L0-2	14	8	2	4	38	22	18
Baginton B L	W4-3	15	9	2	4	42	25	20
Christ Church	L1-3	16	9	2	5	43	28	20
Sherbourne Res	W6-0	17	10	2	5	49	28	22
	D	18	10	3	5			23
	L	19	10	3	6			23
	L	20	10	3	7	55	39	23
	W	21	11	3	7			25
	L	22	11	3	8	67	46	25
	L1-2	23	11	3	9	68	48	25
Veterans	D2-2	24	11	4	9	70	50	26

Coventry and District (Saturday) Football League
Division 1 Table 1965/66

	P	W	D	L	F	A	Pts
St Lukes	21	19	2	0	84	15	40
Meadway Rovers	22	17	1	4	76	26	35
Fillongley	22	15	1	6	60	34	31
Meriden Rovers	22	12	2	8	63	57	26
Folly Lane	22	10	4	8	85	56	24
Stoke Aldermoor	22	9	4	9	54	60	22
Unicorn Celtic	22	9	3	10	68	61	21
Tile Hill Old Boys	22	8	5	9	49	50	21
Moseley United	**22**	**8**	**4**	**10**	**58**	**52**	**20**
Howitzers OC	21	5	2	14	45	77	12
Beechwood Reserves	22	4	2	16	40	84	10
Balsall & Berkswell	22	0	0	22	21	129	0

Section 'A' Table 1965/66

	P	W	D	L	F	A	Pts
Tile Hill OB Reserves	24	19	4	1	80	30	42
Christ Church	24	17	2	5	82	39	36
Sherwyn Ath. Reserves	24	13	5	6	63	43	31
Whexford United	24	12	4	8	79	57	28
Moseley Utd Reserves	**24**	**11**	**4**	**9**	**70**	**50**	**26**
YCW	24	10	5	9	59	68	25
Jubilee Athletic	24	10	2	12	60	63	22
Sherbourne OB Res	24	8	6	10	54	59	22
Brassworkers Reserves	24	10	1	13	60	94	21
Avondale	24	9	2	13	53	52	14
Baginton British Legion	24	7	4	13	43	54	13
Veterans FC	24	3	6	15	46	88	10
Whoberley Wand Res	24	3	3	18	36	86	9

Moseley United FC
Coventry and District (Saturday) Football League
Division 1 Results 1966/67

Opponents	Res	P	W	D	L	F	A	Pts
Howitzers	W8-2	1	1	0	0	8	2	2
Saunders Hall	W5-0	2	2	0	0	13	2	4
Howitzers	W10-1	3	3	0	0	23	3	6
Fillongley	W2-0	4	4	0	0	25	3	8
Clarkson Sports	D3-3	5	4	1	0	28	6	9
Stoke Aldermoor	L0-3	6	4	1	1	28	9	9
Tile Hill O.B.	W2-1	7	5	1	1	30	10	11
St Lukes	L3-6	8	5	1	2	33	16	13
Stoke Aldermoor	W2-0	9	6	1	2	35	16	13
Meriden Rovers	W4-1	10	7	1	2	39	17	15
Folly Lane	L1-2	11	7	1	3	40	19	15
Fillongley	L2-3	12	7	1	4	42	22	15
St Lukes	L0-1	13	7	1	5	42	23	15
Clarkson Sports	L0-1	14	7	1	6	42	24	15
Saunders Hall	D1-1	15	7	2	6	43	25	16
Sherwyn Albion	W2-1	16	8	2	6	45	26	18
Tile Hill O.B	W1-0	17	9	2	6	46	26	20
Folly Lane	L1-2	18	9	2	7	47	28	20
Sherwyn Albion	W2-1	19	10	2	7	49	29	22
Meriden Rovers	W4-0	20	11	2	7	53	29	24
Unicorn Celtic	L1-2	21	11	2	8	54	31	24
Meadway Rvrs.	L2-3	22	11	2	9	56	34	24
Unicorn Celtic	L	23	11	2	10			24
Meadway Rvrs.	L	24	11	2	11	58	39	24

Moseley United Reserves
Coventry and District (Saturday) Football League
Section 'A' Results 1966/67

Opponents	Res	P	W	D	L	F	A	Pts
Jubilee Athletic	W5-1	1	1	0	0	5	1	2
Whexford	L1-3	2	1	0	1	6	4	2
FC Olympic	W5-0	3	2	0	1	11	4	4
Star & Garter	W3-2	4	3	0	1	14	6	6
Trinity United	W5-4	5	4	0	1	19	10	8
Rayon Rangers	L1-3	6	4	0	2	20	13	8
Unicorn Celtic Rs	L2-4	7	4	0	3	22	17	8
Star & Garter	D2-2	8	4	1	3	24	19	9
FC Olympic	W3-1	9	5	1	3	27	20	11
St James 'A'	L1-3	10	5	1	4	28	23	11
Stoke Ald'r Res	D2-2	11	5	2	4	30	25	12
Trinity United	W5-4	12	6	2	4	35	29	14
Homefire Plant	W2-1	13	7	2	4	37	30	16
Whexford	D0-0	14	7	3	4	37	30	17
897 Club	W7-2	15	8	3	4	44	32	19
Barras Green	L0-9	16	8	3	5	44	41	19
YCW Reserves	D0-0	17	8	4	5	44	41	20
Barras Green	L0-2	18	8	4	6	44	43	20
Stoke Ald'r Res	D2-2	19	8	5	6	51	47	21
Homefire Plant	W2-0	20	9	5	6	53	47	23
St James 'A'	W	21	10	5	6		47	24
897 Club	W	22	11	5	6	56	47	26
Jubilee Athletic	W4-3	23	12	5	6	60	50	28
YCW Reserves	D2-2	24	12	6	6	62	52	29
Unicorn Celtic Rs	L3-4	25	12	6	7	65	56	30
Rayon Rangers	L2-7	26	12	6	8	67	63	30

Coventry and District (Saturday) Football League
Division 1 Table 1966/67

	P	W	D	L	F	A	Pts
Clarksons Sports	24	20	1	3	89	41	41
Fillongley	24	16	4	4	75	33	36
St Lukes	24	14	3	7	60	47	31
Folly Lane	24	12	5	7	53	49	29
Stoke Aldermoor	24	10	8	6	61	47	28
Saunders Hall	24	9	8	7	54	52	26
Moseley United	**24**	**11**	**2**	**11**	**58**	**39**	**24**
Unicorn Celtic	24	8	7	9	49	55	23
Meadway Rovers	24	9	3	12	52	47	21
Tile Hill O B	24	9	3	12	45	49	21
Sherwyn Albion	24	3	6	15	35	60	12
Meriden Rovers	24	5	1	18	45	85	11
Howitzers OC	24	2	5	17	23	93	9

Coventry and District (Saturday) Football League
Section 'A' Table 1966/67

	P	W	D	L	F	A	Pts
Unicorn Celtic Rs	26	22	3	1	117	36	47
Barras Green	26	21	1	4	105	37	43
Rayon Rangers	26	16	4	6	103	43	36
Whexford United	26	16	3	7	88	50	35
St James 'A'	26	13	5	8	58	54	31
Moseley Utd Res	**26**	**12**	**6**	**8**	**67**	**63**	**30**
YCW Res	26	12	3	11	84	70	27
Stoke Ald'r Res.	26	11	4	11	66	48	26
Homefire Plant	26	12	2	13	69	65	26
Trinity United	26	8	3	15	69	78	19
FC Olympic	26	8	2	16	65	98	18
Jubilee Athletic R	26	5	2	19	47	91	12
Star and Garter	26	4	4	18	47	94	12
897 Club	26	1	1	24	25	181	3

Moseley United FC
Coventry and District (Saturday) Football League
Division 1 Results 1967/68

Opponents	Res	P	W	D	L	F	A	Pts
Saunders Hall	D2-2	1	0	1	0	2	2	1
Saunders Hall	L0-1	2	0	1	1	2	3	1
Meadway Rvrs.	L0-2	3	0	1	2	2	5	1
Tile Hill O.B.	L0-1	4	0	1	3	2	6	1
Unicorn Celtic	L0-1	5	0	1	4	2	7	1
Meadway Rvrs.	W3-0	6	1	1	4	5	7	3
Stoke Aldermoor	W2-1	7	2	1	4	7	8	5
	L	8	2	1	5			5
Stoke Aldermoor	L1-2	9	2	1	6			5
St James	L2-3	10	2	1	7			5
Tile Hill O.B.	D2-2	11	2	2	7			6
Clarkson Sports	L2-3	12	2	2	8			6
St Lukes	L3-4	13	2	2	9			6
Ryton United	L1-4	14	2	2	10			6
Sherwyn Albion	D1-1	15	2	3	10			7
Sherwyn Albion	W2-0	16	3	3	10			9
St Lukes	W5-1	17	4	3	10			11
YCW	L0-2	18	4	3	11			11
YCW	L1-2	19	4	3	12			11
Fillongley	W3-1	20	5	3	12			13
Unicorn Celtic	W2-1	21	6	3	12			15
	L	22	6	3	13			15
	L	23	6	3	14			15
St James	L1-2	24	6	3	15	39	52	15

The missing results must have been heavy defeats!

Moseley United Reserves
Coventry and District (Saturday) Football League
Section 'A' Results 1967/68

Opponents	Res	P	W	D	L	F	A	Pts
Leofric United	L0-3	1	0	0	1	0	3	0
St James 'A'	D3-3	2	0	1	1	3	6	1
Exhall Youth	L0-1	3	0	1	2	3	7	1
Henley College	D2-2	4	0	2	2	5	9	2
Avondale	L1-5	5	0	2	3	6	14	2
Baginton B L	L1-7	6	0	2	4	7	21	2
Stoke Ald'r Res	L1-5	7	0	2	5	8	26	2
Homefire Plant	L0-4	8	0	2	6	8	30	2
Homefire Plant	D3-3	9	0	3	6	11	33	3
Henley College	W2-1	10	1	3	6	13	34	5
Exhall Youth	L1-2	11	1	3	7	14	36	5
Avondale	L1-4	12	1	3	8	15	40	5
Stoke Ald'r Res	D3-3	13	1	4	8	18	43	6
Leofric United	W6-0	14	2	4	8	24	43	8
St Mary Magd'ne	L1-4	15	2	4	9	25	47	8
St Mary Magd'ne	D2-2	16	2	5	9	27	49	9
St James 'A'	L0-2	17	2	5	10	27	51	9
Baginton B L	L1-7	18	2	5	11	28	58	9

Goals For and Against do not agree with final table.
YCW Reserves resigned from the league in March 1968; records were deleted.

Coventry and District (Saturday) Football League
Division 1 Table 1967/68

	P	W	D	L	F	A	Pts
Saunders Hall	24	19	3	2	71	32	41
Clarksons Sports	24	18	2	4	74	36	38
St James	24	14	5	5	59	41	33
Fillongley	24	15	2	7	64	50	29
YCW	24	14	1	9	64	45	28
Meadway Rovers	24	13	2	9	66	47	26
Stoke Aldermoor	24	9	4	11	53	58	24
Sherwyn Albion	24	9	2	13	52	62	23
Tile Hill O B	24	7	4	13	45	67	21
Unicorn Celtic	24	7	3	14	48	67	21
Moseley United	**24**	**6**	**3**	**15**	**39**	**52**	**12**
Ryton United	24	5	3	16	43	71	11
St Lukes	24	1	4	19	31	80	9

Section 'A' Table 1967/68

	P	W	D	L	F	A	Pts
St Mary Magd'ne	18	12	4	2	64	28	28
St James 'A'	18	12	3	3	50	24	27
Baginton B L	18	11	4	3	64	36	26
Avondale	18	9	2	7	57	48	20
Homefire Plant	18	7	4	7	48	51	18
Exhall Youth	18	8	1	9	30	39	17
Stoke Ald'r Res.	18	5	6	7	40	47	16
Leofric United	18	2	6	10	37	70	10
Henley College	18	2	5	11	35	52	9
Moseley Utd Res	**18**	**2**	**5**	**11**	**29**	**59**	**9**

Moseley United FC
Coventry and District (Saturday) Football League
Division 1 Results 1968/69

Opponents	Res	P	W	D	L	F	A	Pts
Tile Hill O.B.	D2-2	1	0	1	0	2	2	1
Fillongley	W3-1	2	1	1	0	5	3	3
Sherwyn Albion	D3-3	3	1	2	0	8	6	4
Beechwood	W3-1	4	2	2	0	11	7	6
Phildown Dyn.	W1-0	5	3	2	0	12	7	8
Meadway Rvrs.	L2-4	6	3	2	1	14	11	8
Tile Hill O.B.	D1-1	7	3	3	1	15	12	9
Beechwood	L1-3	8	3	3	2	16	15	9
Coachmakers	L0-3	9	3	3	3	16	18	9
Leam Celtic	D2-2	10	3	4	3	18	20	10
Leam Celtic	L0-6	11	3	4	4	18	26	10
YCW	D1-1	12	3	5	4	19	27	11
	D0-0	13	3	6	4	19	27	12
St James	W4-0	14	4	6	4	23	27	14
Sherwyn Albion	L1-3	15	4	6	5	24	30	14
Stoke Alderm'r	W3-0	16	5	6	5	27	30	16
	L	17	5	6	6	27	33	16
	W	18	6	6	6			18
	D	19	6	7	6			19
	L	20	6	7	7	30	35	19
Stoke Alderm'r	L0-3	21	6	7	8	30	38	19
	D	22	6	8	8			20
	D	23	6	9	8			21
St James	W	24	7	9	8	35	42	23

Moseley United Reserves
Coventry and District (Saturday) Football League
Section 'A' Results 1968/69

Opponents	Res	P	W	D	L	F	A	Pts
	W	1	1	0	0			2
	L	2	1	0	1	5	6	2
Henley Coll Res	W3-2	3	2	0	1	8	8	4
YCW Reserves	W3-0	4	3	0	1	11	8	6
Homefire Plant	W3-2	5	4	0	1	14	10	8
Exhall Youth	L2-5	6	4	0	2	16	15	8
Newtown Rgrs	W2-0	7	5	0	2	18	15	10
Avondale	L0-5	8	5	0	3	18	20	10
Whitemoor	L1-2	9	5	0	4	19	22	10
Exhall Youth	L1-3	10	5	0	5	20	25	10
Sherwyn Alb R	L1-2	11	5	0	6	21	27	10
Stoke Aldm'r R	L1-7	12	5	0	7	22	34	10*
	W2-1	13	6	0	7	24	35	12*
Newtown Rgr's	W5-1	14						
YCW Reserves	L0-1	15						
Meriden Rvrs. R	D3-3	16						
Whitemoor	L0-2	17						
	D	18	6	3	9	33	44	15*
Avondale	L1-2	19						
Sherwyn Alb R	L1-3	20						
Henley Coll Res	W6-2	21						
Homefire Plant	L2-3	22	9	3	10	46	51	21*

Definite errors in this list, but data shown * agrees with tables printed in 'The Pink'

Coventry and District (Saturday) Football League
Division 1 Table 1968/69

	P	W	D	L	F	A	Pts
Leam.Celtic	24	17	3	4	95	36	37
Coachmakers	24	15	5	4	73	32	35
Beechwood	24	14	4	6	67	44	32
St James	24	13	4	7	54	37	30
Fillongley	24	13	2	9	59	45	28
YCW	24	10	6	8	50	42	26
Meadway Rvrs	24	11	3	10	58	66	25
Stoke Alderm'r	24	10	4	10	57	52	24
Moseley United	**24**	**7**	**9**	**8**	**35**	**42**	**23**
Henley College	24	9	4	11	39	53	22
Phildown Dyn's	24	5	2	17	47	95	12
Sherwyn Albion	24	4	3	17	41	86	11
Tile Hill O B's	24	2	3	19	39	84	7

Coventry and District (Saturday) Football League
Section 'A' Table 1968/69

	P	W	D	L	F	A	Pts
Exhall	22	16	4	2	62	25	36
Stoke Ald'r Res.	22	16	2	4	81	38	34
Cheylesmore	22	12	5	5	69	37	29
Whitemoor	22	12	5	5	52	34	29
Avondale	22	9	3	10	54	54	21
YCW Reserves	22	8	5	9	42	45	21
Moseley Utd Res	**22**	**9**	**3**	**10**	**46**	**51**	**21**
Henley Coll Res.	22	8	4	10	49	57	20
Homefire Plant	22	6	3	13	45	52	15
Sherwyn Alb Res.	22	5	5	12	35	71	15
Newtown Rangers	22	4	4	14	30	68	12
Meriden Rvs Res.	22	3	5	14	33	62	11

Moseley United Colts
Coventry and District (Saturday) Football League
Section 'B' Results 1968/69

Opponents	Res	P	W	D	L	F	A	Pts
Warwick Youth	L3-4	1	0	0	1	3	4	0
Leam. Celtic R	L3-9	2	0	0	2	6	13	0
Warwick Youth	L2-3	3	0	0	3	8	16	0
Copsewood	W5-2	4	1	0	3	13	18	2
Copsewood	L1-3	5	1	0	4	14	21	2
Homefire Res.	W7-2	6	2	0	4	21	23	4
Phildown Res	W5-1	7	3	0	4	26	24	6
Whexford Res.	W9-0	8	4	0	4	35	24	8
Whoberley Res.	W9-1	9	5	0	4	44	25	10
Grayswood Utd.	W7-1	10	6	0	4	51	26	12
Keresley Celtic	W15-0	11	7	0	4	66	26	14
Keresley Celtic	W7-0	12	8	0	4	73	26	16
Whexford Res.	W8-1	13	9	0	4	81	27	18
Grayswood Utd.	L2-3	14	9	0	5	83	30	18
Whoberley Res.	W4-2	15	10	0	5	87	32	20
Homefire Res.	W2-1	16	11	0	5	89	33	22
Phildown Res.	W7-0	17	12	0	5	96	33	24
Leam Celtic R	L3-6	18	12	0	6	99	39	24

Moseley United Colts
Coventry and District (Saturday) Football League
Section 'B' Table 1968/69

	P	W	D	L	F	A	Pts
Warwick Yth	18	16	1	1	93	34	33
Leam. Celtic R	18	15	1	2	95	28	31
Moseley Colts	**18**	**12**	**0**	**6**	**99**	**39**	**24**
Copsewood	18	9	2	7	51	45	20
Whoberley Res	18	8	3	7	51	60	19
Grayswood Utd	18	8	0	10	45	58	16
Homefire Res	18	5	1	12	45	76	11
Phildown Res	18	4	2	12	41	74	10
Whexford Res	18	2	5	11	38	78	9
Keresley Celtic	18	2	3	13	36	102	7

Moseley United FC
Coventry and District (Saturday) Football League
Division 1 Results 1969/70

Opponents	Res	P	W	D	L	F	A	Pts
Coachmakers	L3-4	1	0	0	1	3	4	0
St James	W4-2	2	1	0	1	7	6	2
Beechwood	D2-2	3	1	1	1	9	8	3
Whitnash	D0-0	4	1	2	1	9	8	4
Leam Celtic	L1-3	5	1	2	2	10	11	4
YCW	L1-3	6	1	2	3	11	14	4
Stoke Alderm'r	L3-7	7	1	2	4	14	21	4
Meadway Rvrs	W4-2	8	2	2	4	18	23	6
Meadway Rvrs	W4-3	9	3	2	4	22	26	8
Hen Lane Soc.	L1-2	10	3	2	5	23	28	8
Leam Celtic	L1-9	11	3	2	6	24	37	8
	L0-1	12	3	2	7	24	38	8
Hen Lane Soc.	W2-1	13	4	2	7	26	39	10
YCW	W3-2	14	5	2	7	29	41	12
Fillongley	L0-6	15	5	2	8	29	47	12
Stoke Alderm'r	W1-0	16	6	2	8	30	47	14
	W4-2	17	7	2	8	34	49	16
	W3-2	18	8	2	8	37	51	18
	L0-2	19	8	2	9	37	53	18
	L1-4	20	8	2	10	38	57	18

Moseley United Reserves
Coventry and District (Saturday) Football League
Section 'A' Results 1969/70

Opponents	Res	P	W	D	L	F	A	Pts
GEC Brit Leg.	L1-5	1	0	0	1	1	5	0
Rowleys Green	L0-7	2	0	0	2	1	12	0
Cheylesmore	L0-5	3	0	0	3	1	17	0
Homefire Plant	L1-5	4	0	0	4	2	22	0
Henley College	L0-4	5	0	0	5	2	26	0
Coombe Social	L0-4	6	0	0	6	2	30	0
Rowleys Green	L0-9	7	0	0	7	2	39	0
Hen Lane Res.	L0-16	8	0	0	8	2	55	0
Leam Celtic R	L3-7	9	0	0	9	5	62	0
Homefire Plant	L2-4	10	0	0	10	7	66	0
Avondale	L0-8	11	0	0	11	7	74	0
Henley College	L3-5	12	0	0	12	10	79	0
	L	13	0	0	13			0
	L	14	0	0	14			0
	L	15	0	0	15	13	95	0
GEC Brit Leg.	L1-4	16	0	1	15	14	99	1
Leam Celtic R	D1-1	17	0	1	16	15	100	1
	L0-8	18	0	1	17	15	108	1

Desperate times, how can you not win one game?!
Missing results must be heavy defeats!
Can you fill in the gaps? No don't bother!

Coventry and District (Saturday) Football League
Division 1 Table 1969/70

	P	W	D	L	F	A	Pts
Leam Celtic	20	15	2	3	83	36	32
YCW	20	12	5	3	48	38	29
Whitnash	20	10	7	3	49	30	27
Fillongley	20	10	5	5	52	31	25
Coachmakers	20	10	1	9	44	36	21
Moseley Utd	**20**	**8**	**2**	**10**	**38**	**57**	**18**
Stoke Ald'r	20	7	2	11	49	64	16
Beechwood	20	7	2	11	38	52	16
St James	20	5	4	11	28	36	14
Hen Lane	20	5	4	11	31	48	14
Meadway Rvs	20	2	4	14	38	71	8

Section 'A' Table 1969/70

	P	W	D	L	F	A	Pts
Henley Coll R	18	15	3	0	60	25	33
Rowley Green	18	14	1	3	79	38	29
Coombe Social	18	13	3	2	53	22	29
Avondale	18	7	2	9	46	48	16
GEC B L	18	7	2	9	47	55	16
Hen Lane Res	18	6	3	9	56	43	15
Leam. Celtic R.	18	6	3	9	43	62	15
Cheylesmore	18	5	3	10	39	43	13
Homefire Plant	18	5	3	10	41	54	13
Moseley Utd R	**18**	**0**	**1**	**17**	**15**	**108**	**1**

A C Godiva

Coventry and District (Sunday) Football League
Senior Division 3 Results 1967/68

Opponents	Res	P	W	D	L	F	A	Pts
Close Athletic	W3-1	1	1	0	0	3	1	2
Rugby Medina	L3-3	2	1	1	0	6	4	3
Courtiers	W1-0	3	2	1	0	7	4	5
Telephone Area	W6-0	4	3	1	0	13	4	9
Colwyn Villa	L2-4	5	3	1	1	15	8	9
Phoenix Royal	L2-3	6	3	1	2	17	11	9
Courtiers	W3-1	7	4	1	2	20	12	11
Phoenix Royal	W2-0	8	5	1	2	22	12	13
Cov. Railwaymn	D1-1	9	5	2	2	23	13	14
Telephone Area	D1-1	10	5	3	2	24	14	15
Rugby Medina	W7-0	11	6	3	2	31	14	17
Close Athletic	W5-0	12	7	3	2	36	14	19
Cov Railwaymn	L0-2	13	7	3	3	36	16	19
Colwyn Villa	L0-1	14	7	3	4	36	17	19
Cov Climax*	D	15	7	4	4			20
Cov Climax*	W	16	8	4	4	41	23	20

*Scores not known.

A C Godiva
Coventry and District (Sunday) Football League
Senior Division 2 Results 1968/69

Opponents	Res	P	W	D	L	F	A	Pts
Youell Athletic	L0-1	1	0	0	1	0	1	0
Courtiers	L0-4	2	0	0	2	0	5	0
Riverside	D2-2	3	0	1	2	2	7	1
Colwyn Villa	L0-2	4	0	1	3	2	9	1
Cov. Railwaymn	W6-1	5	1	1	3	8	10	3
Riverside	W5-1	6	2	1	3	13	11	5
Phoenix Royal	W4-1	7	3	1	3	17	12	7
Parkstone 'B'	W5-2	8	4	1	3	22	14	9
Machin Athletic	L1-4	9	4	1	4	23	18	9
Parkstone 'B'	W2-1	10	5	1	4	25	19	11
Courtiers	W10-1	11	6	1	4	35	20	13
Machin Athletic	L0-7	12	6	1	5	35	27	13
Phoenix Royal	L0-11	13	6	1	6	35	38	13
Cov Railwaymn	D0-0	14	6	2	6	35	38	14
Youell Athletic	W1-0	15	7	2	6	36	38	26
Colwyn Villa	L0-2	16	7	2	7	36	40	16
Cov Climax	W*	17	8	2	7			18
Cov Climax	W*	18	9	2	7	43	43	20

*Scores not known

Coventry and District (Sunday) Football League
Division 3 Table 1967/68

	P	W	D	L	F	A	Pts
Cov Railwaymen	16	11	3	2	65	20	25
Colwyn Villa	16	11	3	2	52	21	25
A C Godiva	**16**	**8**	**4**	**4**	**41**	**23**	**20**
Phoenix Royal	16	9	2	5	36	31	20
Cov Climax	16	7	3	6	51	36	17
Courtiers	16	6	2	8	25	39	14
Telephone Area	16	4	1	11	25	57	9
Rugby Medina	16	3	1	12	30	63	7
Close Athletic	16	3	0	13	32	47	6

Keresley Bell expelled from league, records deleted.

Division 2 Table 1968/69

	P	W	D	L	F	A	Pts
Youell Athletic	17	14	2	1	61	35	30
Colwyn Villa	18	12	3	3	64	21	27
Machin Athletic	18	12	2	4	101	47	26
Cov Railwaymen	18	9	5	4	69	38	23
A C Godiva	**18**	**9**	**2**	**7**	**43**	**43**	**20**
Cov Climax	17	7	1	9	43	47	15
Parkstone 'B'	18	6	2	10	40	46	14
Riverside	18	4	2	12	37	74	10
Phoenix Royal	16	2	2	12	38	72	6
Courtiers	16	0	3	13	17	71	3

Parkstone WMC 'A'
Coventry and District (Sunday) Football League
Senior Division 1 Results 1969/70

Opponents	Result	P	W	D	L	F	A	Pts
Radford Rd Utd.	D0-0	1	0	1	0	0	0	1
Golden Cross	W9-2	2	1	1	0	9	2	3
Lentons Lane	D1-1	3	1	2	0	10	3	4
S C New Star	W5-1	4	2	2	0	15	4	6
Awson Sports	W4-1	5	3	2	0	19	5	8
Cov Railwaym's	W3-1	6	4	2	0	22	6	10
Pinley	W2-1	7	5	2	0	24	7	12
A C Godiva	W10-1	8	6	2	0	34	8	14
Colwyn Villa	W1-0	9	7	2	0	35	8	16
S C New Star	W3-1	10	8	2	0	38	9	18
Golden Cross	D2-2	11	8	3	0	40	11	19
Lentons Lane	W3-0	12	9	3	0	43	11	21
Wheel Wander's	D1-1	13	9	4	0	44	12	22
Wheel Wander's	W5-0	14	10	4	0	49	12	24
Dolphin Ath.	L3-4	15	10	4	1	52	16	24
A C Godiva	W8-0	16	11	4	1	60	16	26
Colwyn Villa	W6-0	17	12	4	1	66	16	28
Dolphin Ath.	L1-6	18	12	4	2	67	22	28
Radford Rd Utd.	W*	19	13	4	2			30
Cov Railwaym's	W*	20	14	4	2	80	24	32

*Scores not known
League table shows 15 wins and 3 draws!

Parkstone WMC 'B'
Coventry and District (Sunday) Football League
Senior Division 2 Results 1969/70

Opponents	Result	P	W	D	L	F	A	Pts
Mortlake	L1-3	1	0	0	1	1	3	0
Cov Climax 'B'	L1-3	2	0	0	2	2	6	0
West End Club	L1-2	3	0	0	3	3	8	0
Spartak	L1-8	4	0	0	4	4	16	0
Moss XI	L1-2	5	0	0	5	5	18	0
Four Provinces	W5-2	6	1	0	5	10	20	2
S C Allesley	D2-2	7	1	1	5	12	22	3
GEC Electronics	W8-0	8	2	1	5	20	22	5
Charterhouse	L0-2	9	2	1	6	20	24	5
Shakespeare	D1-1	10	2	2	6	21	25	6
Cov Climax 'B'	W6-0	11	3	2	6	27	25	8
	L2-3	12	3	2	7	29	28	8
Biggin Hall	W2-0	13	4	2	7	31	28	10
	D3-3	14	4	3	7	34	31	11
Hampton in Ard	W7-0	15	5	3	7	41	31	13
Hampton in Ard	W12-0	16	6	3	7	53	31	15
	L3-4	17	6	3	8	56	35	15
West End Club	W1-0	18	7	3	8	57	35	17
	W	19	8	3	8			19
	D	20	8	4	8			20
	W	21	9	4	8			22
	W	22	10	4	8	69	43	24

Biggin Hall replaced Four Provinces half way through the season.

Senior Division 1 Table 1969/70
Coventry and District (Sunday) Football League

	P	W	D	L	F	A	Pts
Dolphin Athletic	20	17	2	1	88	27	36
Parkstone 'A'	**20**	**15**	**3**	**2**	**80**	**24**	**33**
Lentons Lane	20	13	5	2	68	29	31
S C New Star	20	10	2	8	56	55	22
Pinley	20	9	3	8	52	41	21
Wheel Wand'rs	20	9*	6*	6*	44	37	21*
Golden Cross	20	7	4	9	40	65	18
Colwyn Villa	20	5	4	11	44	50	14
Awson Sports	20	5	3	12	37	50	13
Cov Railwaym's	20	3	3	14	28	59	9
A C Godiva	20	0	0	20	16	116	0

*The W D and L results do not tally with the Points total

Senior Division 2 Table 1969/70
Coventry and District (Sunday) Football League

	P	W	D	L	F	A	Pts
Shakespeare	22	17	3	2	75	22	37
Mortlake	22	15	4	3	83	37	34
Spartak	22	16	1	5	82	24	31
Parkstone 'B'	**22**	**10**	**4**	**8**	**69**	**43**	**24**
Moss XI	22	8	7	7	65	50	23
Cov Climax 'B'	22	11	1	10	67	60	23
Charterhouse	22	9	4	9	51	44	22
West End Club	22	8	4	10	60	53	20
GEC Electronics	22	7	4	11	51	64	18
S C Allesley 'B'	22	5	8	9	46	64	18
Biggin Hall	22	3	2	17	30	105	8
Hampton	22	2	0	20	23	134	1

Parkstone WMC 'A'

Coventry and District (Sunday) Football League
Premier Division 2 Results 1970/71

Opponents	Res	P	W	D	L	F	A	Pts
Cov Climax	D1-1	1	0	1	0	1	1	1
Stoke Ex-Serv.	L1-2	2	0	1	1	2	3	1
Binley Woods	W3-2	3	1	1	1	5	5	3
Whitley Ams.	L1-2	4	1	1	2	6	7	3
Unbrako	W4-3	5	2	1	2	10	10	5
Dolphin Ath.	W1-0	6	3	1	2	11	10	7
	L	7	3	1	3			7
	D	8	3	2	3			8
	W	9	4	2	3			10
	L	10	4	2	4	19	27	10
Albany Social	L2-3	11	4	2	5	21	30	10
Dolphin Ath.	D2-2	12	4	3	5	23	32	11
Cov Climax	W5-0	13	5	3	5	28	32	13
Dunchurch	L2-4	14	5	3	6	30	36	13
Albany Social	W4-3	15	6	3	6	34	39	15
Stoke Ex-Serv.	L0-3	16	6	3	7	34	42	15

Rugby Rangers quit the league in December, and Coventry Colliery resigned in April.

Parkstone WMC 'B'
Coventry and District (Sunday) Football League
Senior Division 2 Results 1970/71

Opponents	Res	P	W	D	L	F	A	Pts
	W1-0	1	1	0	0	1	0	2
Buncranna	L0-4	2	1	0	1	1	4	2
GEC Electronics	W4-3	3	2	0	1	5	7	4
Cov Nomads	D2-2	4	2	1	1	7	9	5
Pegasus	W4-2	5	3	1	1	11	11	7
S C Allesley	W5-4	6	4	1	1	16	15	9
Cov Climax 'B'	W10-2	7	5	1	1	26	17	11
Ernesford Gr.	W3-2	8	6	1	1	29	19	13
Greyfriars	W7-1	9	7	1	1	36	20	15
	W	10	8	1	1			17
	W	11	9	1	1			19
Cov Climax 'B'	W11-0	12	10	1	1			21
Buncranna	W7-0	13	11	1	1			23
	W	14	12	1	1	72	28	25
GEC Electronics	W8-4	15	13	1	1	80	32	27
Veterans 65	W5-2	16	14	1	1	85	34	29
Charterhouse	W3-2	17	15	1	1	88	36	31
S C Allesley	D3-3	18	16	2	1	91	39	33
Ernesford Gr.	W7-2	19	16	2	1	98	41	34
Pegasus	L0-2	20	16	2	2	98	43	34
Veterans 65	W6-0	21	17	2	2	104	43	36
Barras WMC	W6-1	22	18	2	2	110	44	38

Premier Division 2 Table 1970/71
Coventry and District (Sunday) Football League

	P	W	D	L	F	A	Pts
Dunchurch	16	14	0	2	71	17	28
Stoke Ex-Service	15	14	0	1	62	20	28
Whitley Wander's	16	10	3	3	49	16	23
Albany Social	16	7	2	7	41	49	16
Parkstone 'A'	**16**	**6**	**3**	**7**	**34**	**42**	**15**
Dolphin Athletic	16	6	2	8	37	40	14
Unbrako	15	5	1	9	38	62	11
Binley Woods	16	1	3	12	17	53	5
Cov Climax	16	0	2	14	18	72	3

Rugby Rangers quit the league in December, and Coventry Colliery resigned in April and their records were deleted.

Senior Division 2 Table 1970/71
Coventry and District (Sunday) Football League

	P	W	D	L	F	A	Pts
Parkstone 'B'	**22**	**18**	**2**	**2**	**110**	**44**	**38**
Buncranna Hearts	22	18	2	2	105	42	38
S C Allesley	21	14	4	3	84	41	32
Chaterhouse	22	13	5	4	63	35	31
Pegasus	22	11	4	7	60	43	26
Cov Nomads	22	9	5	8	61	52	23
Barras Green	22	11	0	11	92	59	22
Ernesford	22	6	5	11	58	73	17
GEC Electronics	21	6	1	14	71	75	13
Veterans	21	4	3	14	29	74	11
Greyfriars	22	2	2	18	41	118	8
Climax	21	1	1	19	24	143	3

Parkstone 'B' and Buncranna have identical results and goal averages! A unique situation, they shared the championship for half a season each

Avondale FC
Coventry and District (Saturday) Football League
Section 'A' Results 1970/71

Opponents	Res	P	W	D	L	F	A	Pts
GEC Brit Leg	W	1	1	0	0			2
Hen Lane Res	W	2	2	0	0			4
GEC Brit Leg	W5-1	3	3	0	0	11	3	4
Newtown Rgrs.	D1-1	4	3	1	0	12	4	7
Homefire	W5-0	5	3	1	0	17	4	9
Copsewood	W5-2	6	4	1	0	22	6	11
Doubleday	D4-4	7	4	2	0	26	10	12
Hertford Utd.	W9-3	8	6	2	0	35	13	14
Homefire	W7-1	9	7	2	0	42	14	16
Hen Lane Res.	W6-3	10	8	2	0	48	17	18
Homefire	W3-0	11	9	2	0	51	17	20
Keresdon Park	L1-3	12	10	2	0	52	20	20
Unbrako	W3-1	13	10	2	1	55	21	22
Unbrako	W5-2	14	11	2	1	60	23	24
Hertford Utd.	W10-1	15	12	2	1	70	24	26
Newtown Rgrs.	W3-1	16	13	2	1	73	25	28
Lanchester Col	D3-3	17	13	3	1	76	28	29
Lanchester Col	W3-1	18	14	3	1	79	29	31
Keresdon Park	W5-1	19	15	3	1	84	30	33
Doubleday	L0-3	20	15	3	2	84	33	33

Coventry and District (Saturday) Football League
Section 'A' Table 1970-71

	P	W	D	L	F	A	Pts
Doubleday	20	18	2	0	110	17	38
Avondale FC	**20**	**15**	**3**	**2**	**84**	**33**	**33**
Keresdon Park	20	10	5	5	53	39	25
Lanchester College	20	10	4	6	54	34	24
Newtown Rangers	20	10	3	7	59	47	23
Unbrako	20	10	2	8	60	57	22
Hen Lane Reserves	20	8	3	9	59	52	19
Copsewood	20	7	3	10	46	52	17
Homefire	20	5	1	14	34	64	11
Hertford United	20	1	2	17	30	103	4
GEC British Legion	20	2	0	18	15	101	4

Avondale FC Coventry and District (Saturday) Football League Division 2 Results 1971/72

Opponents	Res	P	W	D	L	F	A	Pts
Foleshill Ath.	W4-0	1	1	0	0	4	0	2
Exhall	W5-3	2	2	0	0	9	3	4
Doubleday	L0-2	3	2	0	1	9	5	4
Motor Panels	W2-1	4	3	0	1	11	6	6
Indian New Star	W2-0	5	4	0	1	13	6	8
Coombe Social	W2-0	6	5	0	1	15	6	10
Meadway Res.	D1-1	7	5	1	1	16	7	11
Meriden Rovers	L3-1	8	6	1	1	19	8	13
Indian Comm.	W2-0	9	7	1	1	21	8	15
Motor Panels	W5-1	10	8	1	1	26	9	17
Doubleday	D1-1	11	8	2	1	27	10	18
Sherwyn Ath.	W3-1	12	9	2	1	30	11	20
Sherwyn Ath.	W2-1	13	10	2	1	32	12	22
Indian Comm.	W2-1	14	11	2	1	34	13	24
Indian New Star	W5-2	15	12	2	1	39	15	26
Meadway Res.	W5-4	16	13	2	1	44	19	28
Stoneleigh	L3-5	17	13	2	2	47	24	28
Rayon Rangers	D3-3	18	13	3	2	50	27	29
Rayon Rangers	W4-1	19	14	3	2	54	28	31
Stoneleigh	W2-1	20	15	3	2	56	29	33
Henley College	W5-1	21	16	3	2	61	30	35
Exhall	L1-2	22	16	3	3	62	32	35
Henley College	W2-1	23	17	3	3	64	33	37
Lyric Athletic	L1-3	24	17	3	4	65	36	37
Meriden Rovers	W2-1	25	18	3	4	67	37	39
Coombe Social	L1-2	26	18	3	5	68	39	39
Foleshill Ath.	L1-3	27	18	3	6	69	42	39
Lyric Athletic	D3-3	28	18	4	6	72	45	40

Coventry and District (Saturday) Football League
Division 2 Table 1971-72

	P	W	D	L	F	A	Pts
Doubleday	28	23	4	1	123	34	50
Indian Comm'wlth	28	25	0	3	120	37	50
Avondale FC	**28**	**18**	**4**	**6**	**72**	**45**	**40**
Rayon Rangers	28	14	7	7	73	52	35
Coombe Social	28	16	1	11	68	62	33
Lyric Athletic	28	11	8	9	63	60	30
Sherwyn Athletic	28	12	5	11	62	62	29
Exhall	27	10	6	11	56	60	26
Indian New Star	28	10	5	13	47	67	25
Foleshill Athletic	28	8	8	12	62	75	24
Meriden Rovers	28	9	5	14	74	73	23
Stoneleigh	28	8	1	19	57	74	17
Meadway Reserves	28	7	3	18	42	94	17
Henley College	27	5	2	20	41	93	12
Motor Panels	28	2	3	23	39	113	7

Avondale FC
Coventry and District (Saturday) Football League
Division 2 Results 1972/73

Opponents	Res	P	W	D	L	F	A	Pts
Exhall	W3-1	1	1	0	0	3	1	2
Sherwyn Ath.	D1-1	2	1	1	0	4	2	3
Exhall	W5-0	3	2	1	0	9	2	5
Stoneleigh	W5-0	4	3	1	0	14	2	7
Lyric Athletic	D1-1	5	3	2	0	15	3	8
Keresdon Park	W3-2	6	4	2	0	18	5	10
India New Star	L0-2	7	4	2	1	18	7	10
Foleshill Ath.	D4-4	8	4	3	1	22	11	11
Rayon Rangers	L2-4	9	4	3	2	24	15	11
Moseley Utd.	W5-1	10	5	3	2	29	16	13
Homefire Plant	L4-7	11	5	3	3	33	23	13
Meriden Rovers	W3-0	12	6	3	3	36	23	15
Coombe Social	D2-2	13	6	4	3	38	25	16
Meadway Res.	W7-1	14	7	4	3	45	26	18
Sherwyn Ath.	D1-1	15	7	5	3	46	27	19
Lyric Athletic	W8-0	16	8	5	3	54	27	21
Moseley Utd.	W2-0	17	9	5	3	56	27	23
Rayon Rangers	W4-0	18	10	5	3	60	27	25
India New Star	W4-2	19	11	5	3	64	29	27
Foleshill Ath.	W2-1	20	12	5	3	66	30	29
Meriden Rovers	L2-3	21	12	5	4	68	33	29
Stoneleigh	W5-0	22	13	5	4	73	33	31
Coombe Social	W5-2	23	14	5	4	78	35	33
Keresdon Park	W3-1	24	15	5	4	81	36	35
Homefire Plant	W2-0	25	16	5	4	83	36	37
Meadway Res.	W2-0	26	17	5	4	85	36	39

Coventry and District (Saturday) Football League
Division 2 Table 1972-73

	P	W	D	L	F	A	Pts
Avondale FC	**26**	**17**	**5**	**4**	**85**	**36**	**39**
Exhall	26	18	3	5	96	56	39
Rayon Rangers	26	15	8	3	73	31	38
Keresdon Park	26	15	3	8	62	40	33
Meriden Rovers	26	13	6	7	71	56	32
Homefire	26	14	3	9	72	60	31
Sherwyn Athletic	26	12	4	10	59	50	28
Indian New Star	26	10	5	11	47	53	25
Foleshill Athletic	26	10	4	12	56	56	24
Coombe Social	26	10	4	12	52	64	24
Meadway Reserves	26	5	5	16	35	68	14
Moseley United	26	3	8	15	38	71	13
Stoneleigh	26	5	3	18	46	84	12
Lyric Athletic	26	1	7	18	32	99	9

Barras Green Rangers
Coventry and District (Sunday) Football League
Senior Division 5 Results 1972/73

Opponents	Res	P	W	D	L	F	A	Pts
Cov AEC	W3-0	1	1	0	0	3	0	2
Stoneleigh	W9-0	2	2	0	0	12	0	4
Sovereign	W10-1	3	3	0	0	22	1	6
Nighthawks	L3-5	4	3	0	1	25	6	6
AC XI	L1-2	5	3	0	2	26	8	6
Stanton WMC	W6-0	6	4	0	2	32	8	8
South United	W2-1	7	5	0	2	34	9	10
Cov AEC	W2-1	8	6	0	2	36	10	12
Stanton WMC	W3-1	9	7	0	2	39	11	14
Devon Wand's	W2-1	10	8	0	2	41	12	16
AC XI	L0-1	11	8	0	3	41	13	16
Unbrako	W10-0	12	9	0	3	51	13	18
Unbrako	W4-2	13	10	0	3	55	15	20
White Bear	W7-2	14	11	0	3	62	17	22
White Bear	W8-3	15	12	0	3	70	20	24
South United	D1-1	16	12	1	3	71	21	25
Daytona Sports	L0-3	17	12	1	4	71	24	25
		18						
		19						
		20						
		21						
		22	13	2	7	92	42	28

Coventry and District (Sunday) Football League
Senior Division 5 Table 1972-73

	P	W	D	L	F	A	Pts
Daytona Sports	22	18	3	1	101	26	39
Nighthawks	22	18	1	3	129	39	37
Devon Wanderers	22	14	3	6	90	35	31
Coventry AEC	22	13	4	5	70	37	30
Barras Gr'n Rangers	**22**	**13**	**2**	**7**	**92**	**42**	**28**
South United	22	9	8	5	66	33	26
A.C. X1	22	9	6	7	78	51	24
Unbrako	22	5	4	13	52	93	14
White Bear	22	4	4	14	39	91	12
Stanton WMC	22	5	2	15	58	98	12
Sovereign	22	4	0	18	19	92	8
Stoneleigh	22	1	1	20	33	149	3

Coventry and Central Warwickshire (Sunday) Football League
Senior Division 3 Table1972-73 Season

	P	W	D	L	F	A	Pts
Padmore Rovers	18	15	2	1	95	14	32
Coronation Club Res.	18	15	0	3	70	17	30
Builder's Club	18	12	2	4	72	34	26
Craven and Binley	18	10	2	6	60	35	22
Corinthians	18	8	2	8	64	52	18
Newtown Athletic	18	8	1	9	51	48	17
Barras Green WMC	**18**	**6**	**1**	**11**	**39**	**60**	**13**
Courthouse	18	5	1	12	29	73	11
Falcon	18	4	1	13	32	68	9
Area Sporting Club	18	1	0	17	13	124	2

Barras Green WMC
Coventry and Central Warwickshire (Sunday) Football League
Senior Division 2 Results 1973/74

Opponents	Res	P	W	D	L	F	A	Pts
Easenhall Utd	W	1	1	0	0	?	0	2
Newtown Ath.	W	2	2	0	0	13	0	4
A L Dunn	W4-2	3	3	0	0	17	2	6
Corinthians	W6-0	4	4	0	0	21	4	8
Standard Bearer	W6-2	5	5	0	0	27	6	10
Coombe Social	W5-1	6	6	0	0	32	7	12
Builders Club	W2-1	7	7	0	0	34	8	14
Midland Rgrs.	W2-1	8	8	0	0	36	9	16
Builders Club	W4-3	9	9	0	0	40	12	18
Courthouse	D2-2	10	9	1	0	42	14	19
Standard Bearer	D1-1	11	9	2	0	43	15	20
Newtown Ath.	W9-1	12	10	2	0	52	16	22
Coombe Social	W7-1	13	11	2	0	59	17	24
A L Dunn	W9-1	14	12	2	0	68	18	26
Midland Rgrs.	D3-3	15	12	3	0	71	21	27
Easenhall Utd.	W7-1	16	13	3	0	78	22	29
Courthouse	L2-3	17	13	3	1	80	25	29
Corinthians	W19-1	18	14	3	1	99	26	31

Coventry and District Sunday Football League
Senior Division 4 Table 1973-74

	P	W	D	L	F	A	Pts
Nighthawks	22	20	0	2	133	25	40
Daytona Sports	22	18	2	2	99	20	38
Devon Wanderers	22	14	5	3	77	32	33
South United	22	14	3	5	58	30	31
Arden Products	22	10	4	8	63	67	24
Gino's XI	22	9	4	9	59	73	22
Coventry AEC	22	9	2	11	56	61	20
Mason United	22	5	3	14	33	74	13
A.C. XI	22	5	2	15	39	55	12
Binley Woods	22	5	1	16	42	91	11
Coventry Ev. Tel.	22	4	2	16	31	93	10
Barras Gr'n Rangers	**22**	**4**	**2**	**18**	**27**	**88**	**8***

*2 points deleted ?

Coventry and Central Warwickshire (Sunday) Football League
Senior Division 2 Table 1973-74 Season

	P	W	D	L	F	A	Pts
Barras Green WMC	**18**	**14**	**3**	**1**	**99**	**26**	**31**
Standard Bearer	18	14	2	2	62	22	30
Midland Bank	18	10	3	4	71	38	23
Newtown Athletic	18	10	3	5	61	61	23
Builder's Club	18	9	2	7	70	46	20
Courthouse	18	7	4	7	32	44	18
AL Dunns	17	6	1	10	41	51	13
Coombe Social	17	6	0	11	41	55	12
Corinthians Whitmore	17	2	0	15	32	112	4
Exhall United	17	0	2	15	19	73	2

Barras Green Rangers
Coventry and District (Saterday) Football League
Section 'B' Table 1974/75

Opponents	Res	P	W	D	L	F	A	Pts
Bubbenhall Res.	W10-0	1	1	0	0	10	0	2
SNR	W8-1	2	2	0	0	18	1	4
New Hillfields	W11-1	3	3	0	0	29	2	6
Edgewick Utd	L1-2	4	3	0	1	30	4	6
Manor Park	W6-4	5	4	0	1	36	8	8
Meriden Res.	W8-0	6	5	0	1	44	8	10
Brookstray	W6-2	7	6	0	1	50	10	12
Bubbenhall Res.	W2-1	8	7	0	1	52	11	14
Tandee 72 Res.	W7-0	9	8	0	1	59	11	16
SNR	W12-1	10	9	0	1	71	12	18
Cheylesmore	W5-0	11	10	0	1	76	12	20
Manor Park	W9-1	12	11	0	1	85	13	22
Cheylesmore	L0-2	13	11	0	2	85	15	22
Meriden Res.	W10-1	14	12	0	2	95	16	24
Edgewick Utd	W5-1	15	13	0	2	100	17	26
New Hillfields	D4-4	16	14	1	2	104	21	27
Tandee 72 Res.	D	17	14	2	2			28
Brookstray	W2-0	18	14	2	2	107	23	30

Confusion ruled at the season end. The League ran a Supplementary Cup competition because most teams had nearly finished their fixtures. Then it rained and rained. To get the fixtures played the Cup and League fixtures were 'doubled up', but didn't separate the results them in 'The Pink'. The only result in doubt is Tandee drawing their last game, as they lost 7-1 to Barras in the Supplemetary Cup.

Barras Green WMC
Coventry and Central Warwickshire (Sunday) Football League
Senior Division 1 Table 1974/75

Opponents	Res	P	W	D	L	F	A	Pts
Newtown Ath.	W8-2	1	1	0	0	8	2	2
Minster Rgrs.	W9-2	2	2	0	0	17	4	4
Brassworkers	W7-1	3	3	0	0	24	5	6
Soc. Services	W3-1	4	4	0	0	27	6	8
Corinthians	W9-0	5	5	0	0	36	6	10
Soc. Services	W4-2	6	6	0	0	40	8	12
Corinthians	W7-0	7	7	0	0	47	8	14
Mowog	W14-1	8	8	0	0	61	9	16
Bridge End Res.	W4-2	9	9	0	0	65	11	18
Glade Res.	W6-1	10	10	0	0	71	12	20
Mowog	W6-3	11	10	0	1	77	15	22
Minster Rgrs.	L1-3	12	11	0	1	78	18	24
Celtic Travellers	W3-0	13	12	0	1	81	18	26
Bridge End Res.	W4-3	14	13	0	1	85	21	28
Celtic Travellers	W3-0	15	14	0	1	88	21	30
Brassworkers	W7-1	16	14	1	1	95*	22*	32
Glade Res.		17						
Newtown Ath.		18						

*Goals For and Against do not agree with League table

Coventry and District (Saturday) Football League
Section 'B' Table 1974-75

	P	W	D	L	F	A	Pts
Edgewick United	18	16	1	1	74	22	33
Barras Gr'n Rangers	**18**	**14**	**2**	**2**	**107**	**23**	**30**
Brookstray	18	10	3	5	59	39	23
Cheylesmore	18	10	2	6	61	49	22
Tandee 72 Reserves	18	9	3	6	55	42	21
New Hillfields	18	7	3	8	57	60	17
Manor Park	17	7	1	10	44	49	15
Meriden Reserves	17	6	1	11	33	75	13
Bubbenhall Reserves	18	4	0	14	37	88	8
SNR	18	0	0	18	14	98	0

Coventry and Central Warwickshire (Sunday) Football League
Senior Division 1 Table 1974-75 Season

	P	W	D	L	F	A	Pts
Barras Green WMC	**16**	**15**	**0**	**1**	**94**	**23**	**30**
Celtic Travellers	18	14	1	3	78	35	29
Brassworkers	18	11	3	4	64	43	25
Social Services	18	11	2	5	55	32	24
Bridge End Res.	18	8	2	8	51	50	18
Minster Rangers	18	6	3	9	40	48	15
Glade	17	4	5	8	41	52	13
Newtown Athletic	17	3	2	12	46	72	8
Corinthians Whitmore	18	2	3	12	35	75	7
Mowog Athletic	18	1	3	14	28	98	6

Barras Green Rangers
Coventry and District (Saturday) Football League
Section 'A' Results 1975/76

Opponents	Res	P	W	D	L	F	A	Pts
	W2-0	1	1	0	0	2	0	2
GEC Sports	W4-1	2	2	0	0	6	1	4
Tile Hill O B	W3-2	3	3	0	0	9	3	6
Phoenix A	W6-0	4	4	0	0	15	3	8
Brookstray	W4-2	5	5	0	0	19	5	10
Cheylesmore	W3-1	6	6	0	0	22	6	12
Self Change Gear	W6-1	7	7	0	0	28	7	14
Phoenix A	W8-1	8	8	0	0	36	8	16
Edgewick United	W3-2	9	9	0	0	39	10	18
Hertford United	W4-1	10	10	0	0	43	11	20
Hall Green	W3-0	11	11	0	0	46	11	22
	W12-0	12	12	0	0	58	11	24
Edgewick United	W2-1	13	13	0	0	60	12	26
Whexford United	W9-0	14	14	0	0	62	12	28
Brookstray	W7-0	15	15	0	0	71	12	30
Tile Hill O B	D1-1	16	15	1	0	72	13	31
GEC Sports	W5-1	17	16	1	0	77	14	33
Hen Lane Res.	W6-3	18	17	1	0	83	17	35
Whexford United	W5-2	19	18	1	0	88	19	37
Hertford United	W5-1	20	19	1	0	93	20	39
Self Change Gear	W8-0	21	20	1	0	101	20	41
Cheylesmore	W5-0	22	21	1	0	106	20*	43

New Union resigned from the league in March – records deleted
*Goals against do not agree with final League table.

Barras Green WMC
Coventry and Central Warwickshire (Sunday) Football League
Premier Division 2 Table 1975/76

Opponents	Res	P	W	D	L	F	A	Pts
	W3-2	1	1	0	0	3	2	2
Brassworkers	W9-1	2	2	0	0	12	3	4
Bubbenhall	W4-2	3	3	0	0	16	5	6
Jules Verne	D4-4	4	3	1	0	20	9	7
Brassworkers	W6-0	5	4	1	0	26	9	9
Glade Res.	W5-3	6	5	1	0	31	12	11
Bubbenhall	W5-1	7	6	1	0	36	13	13
	W3-0	8	7	1	0	39	13	15
Royal Oak	W5-3	9	8	1	0	44	16	17
Glade Res.	W5-0	10	9	1	0	49	16	19
Minster Rgrs.	W4-0	11	10	1	0	53	16	21
Minster Rgrs.	W6-2	12	11	1	0	59	18	23
Reburn Henley	W4-2	13	12	1	0	63	20	25
1925 Club	W7-3	14	13	1	0	70	23	27
Jules Verne	W8-1	15	14	1	0	78	24	29
Celtic Travellers	L2-5	16	14	1	1	80	29	29
Royal Oak	L3-4	17	14	1	2	83	33	29
Redburn Henley	W1-0	18	15	1	2	84	33	31

Coventry and District (Saturday) Football League
Section 'A' Table 1975-76

	P	W	D	L	F	A	Pts
Barras Gr'n Rangers	**22**	**21**	**1**	**0**	**106**	**21**	**43**
Cheylesmore	22	16	2	4	81	32	34
Tile Hill Old Boys	22	11	6	5	81	42	28
Edgewick United	22	13	2	7	65	37	28
Self Change	22	12	3	7	55	48	27
GEC Sports	22	11	1	10	71	60	23
Brookstray	22	8	4	10	44	65	20
Hall Green	22	6	4	12	31	52	16
Hertford United	22	5	3	14	38	71	13
Hen Lane Reserves	22	4	3	15	38	78	11
Whexford United	22	4	3	15	33	82	11
Phoenix	22	3	4	15	27	82	10

Coventry and Central Warwickshire (Sunday) Football League
Premier Division 2 Table 1975-76 Season

	P	W	D	L	F	A	Pts
Barras Green WMC	**18**	**15**	**1**	**2**	**84**	**33**	**30**
Royal Oak	18	13	0	5	70	30	26
Jules Verne Athletic	18	11	4	3	54	41	26
Celtic Travellers	18	9	6	3	63	36	24
Bubbenhall	18	10	4	4	61	35	24
Redburn Henley	18	8	3	7	40	32	19
1925 Club	17	3	3	12	43	65	9
Glade	17	4	1	13	29	63	9
Minster Rangers	18	3	0	15	29	76	6
Brassworkers	18	2	2	14	26	85	6

Apollo Rangers FC
Coventry and District (Sunday) Football League
Senior Division 4 Results 1975/76

Opponents	Res	P	W	D	L	F	A	Pts
Golden Eagle	D0-0	1	0	1	0	0	0	1
Mowog	L0-4	2	0	1	1	0	4	1
Wyken Pippen	L1-2	3	0	1	2	1	6	1
Walsgrave WMC	D2-2	4	0	2	2	3	8	2
Post Office Utd.	W7-0	5	1	2	2	10	8	4
City Treasurers	L2-3	6	1	2	3	12	11	4
Golden Eagle	W3-0	7	2	2	3	15	11	6
Cov. Even. Tel.	L0-2	8	2	2	4	15	13	6
Walsgrave WMC	D3-3	9	2	3	4	18	16	7
Foleshill Social	W3-2	10	3	3	4	21	18	9
AC XI	D1-1	11	3	4	4	22	19	10
Sweeney Todd	L0-2	12	3	4	5	22	21	10
Stoke Cov Club	L0-3	13	3	4	6	22	24	10
Cov. Even. Tel.	W3-0	14	4	4	6	25	24	12
Post Office Utd.	L0-1	15	4	4	7	25	25	12
Stoke Cov Club	L0-4	16	4	4	8	25	29	12
Foleshill Social	W1-0	17	5	4	8	26	29	14
Wyken Pippen	L0-2	18	5	4	9	26	31	14
Sweeney Todd	L1-5	19	5	4	10	27	36	14
AC XI	W3-1	20	6	4	10	30	37	16
Mowog	W5-1	21	7	4	10	35	38	18
City Treasurers	L2-3	22	7	4	11	37	41*	18

*Goals against do not agree with final League table.

Coventry and District (Sunday) Football League
Senior Division 4 Table 1975-76

	P	W	D	L	F	A	Pts
Sweeney Todd	22	22	0	0	131	12	44
Stoke Coventry Club	22	18	1	3	108	26	37
Wyken Pippin	22	14	1	7	60	43	29
AC XI	22	13	2	7	69	44	28
Cov Even. Telegraph	22	11	4	7	52	58	25
City Treasurers	21	10	4	7	54	51	24
Apollo Rangers	**22**	**7**	**4**	**11**	**37**	**42**	**18**
Walsgrave WMC	21	5	5	11	37	70	15
Golden Eagle	21	6	3	12	28	71	15
Mowog	22	5	3	14	36	69	13
Foleshill Social	22	6	1	15	38	81	13
Post Office	22	1	0	21	35	114	2

Apollo Rangers FC
Coventry and District (Sunday) Football League
Senior Division 4 Results 1976/77

Opponents	Res	P	W	D	L	F	A	Pts
Rowen Athletic	W4-1	1	1	0	0	4	1	2
Herberts	D2-2	2	1	1	0	6	3	3
Cov. Even. Tel.	W7-3	3	2	1	0	13	6	5
Mowog	W5-2	4	3	1	0	18	8	7
Pegasus	W12-0	5	4	1	0	30	8	9
Walsgrave WMC	L3-4	6	4	1	1	33	12	9
Godiva Rangers	L1-2	7	4	1	2	34	14	9
Foleshill Social	L1-2	8	4	1	3	35	16	9
City Treasurers	W2-1	9	5	1	3	37	17	11
Rowen Athletic	W2-0	10	6	1	3	39	17	13
Walsgrave WMC	L0-2	11	6	1	4	39	19	13
WMPTE	L1-4	12	6	1	5	40	23	13
Mowog	W4-0	13	7	1	5	44	23	15
Foleshill Social	D1-1	14	7	2	5	45	24	16
WMPTE	L0-1	15	7	2	6	45	25	16
City Treasurers	D1-1	16	7	3	6	46	26	17
Herberts	W5-1	17	8	3	6	51	27	19
Pegasus	W5-0	18	9	3	6	56	27	21
Godiva Rangers	W3-0	19	10	3	6	59	27	23
Whitley Wands.	W3-2	20	11	3	6	62	29	25
Cov. Even. Tel.	W6-3	21	12	3	6	68	32	27
Whitley Wands.	W4-2	22	13	3	6	72	34	29

Coventry and District (Sunday) Football League
Senior Division 4 Table 1976-77

	P	W	D	L	F	A	Pts
Godiva Rangers	17	13	3	1	55	24	29
Cov Even. Telegraph	20	12	4	4	72	46	28
City Treasurers	15	10	3	2	56	21	23
Apollo Rangers	**22**	**13**	**3**	**6**	**72**	**34**	**29**
Herberts	19	8	4	7	63	59	20
Whitley Wanderers	18	8	3	7	61	39	19
WMPTE	18	7	3	8	35	42	17
Foleshill Social	17	4	8	5	37	43	16
Walsgrave WMC	16	7	1	8	44	45	15
Mowog	18	5	4	9	45	43	14
Pegasus	18	2	2	14	21	88	6
Rowen Athletic	16	1	0	15	24	98	2

Not complete!

Apollo Rangers FC
Coventry and District (Sunday) Football League
Senior Division 4 Results 1977/78

Opponents	Res	P	W	D	L	F	A	Pts
Chestnut Villa	W5-2	1	1	0	0	5	2	2
Bridge End	D0-0	2	1	1	0	5	2	3
Walsgrave WMC	W6-0	3	2	1	0	11	2	5
Foleshill Social	D5-5	4	2	2	0	16	7	6
Baginton B.L.	D1-1	5	2	3	0	17	8	7
Mowog	L2-3	6	2	3	1	19	11	7
WMPTE	W7-1	7	3	3	1	26	12	9
Whitley Wands.	W4-2	8	4	3	1	30	14	11
Cov. Even. Tel.	W6-0	9	5	3	1	36	14	13
WMPTE	W2-1	10	6	3	1	38	15	15
Baginton B.L.	L1-6	11	6	3	2	39	21	17
Eastern Green	W4-3	12	7	3	2	43	24	17
Walsgrave WMC	W4-1	13	8	3	2	47	25	19
Henley S&S	L0-2	14	8	3	3	47	27	19
Foleshill Social	W1-0	15	9	3	3	48	27	21
Cov. Even. Tel.	D3-3	16	9	4	3	51	30	22
Whitley Wands.	D0-0	17	9	5	3	51	30	23
Henley S&S	W3-2	18	10	5	3	54	32	25
Chestnut Villa	L2-4	19	10	5	4	56	36	25
Eastern Green	L1-8	20	10	5	5	57	44	25
	W4-0	21	11	5	5	61	44	27
		22						

Not complete!

Coventry and District (Sunday) Football League
Senior Division 4 Table 1977-78

	P	W	D	L	F	A	Pts
Eastern Green	22	19	2	1	89	21	40
Mowog	21	18	1	2	87	30	37
Baginton	21	14	5	2	74	28	33
Apollo Rangers	**21**	**11**	**5**	**5**	**61**	**44**	**27**
Henley S&S	21	10	2	9	64	51	22
Chestnut Villa	22	10	1	11	47	52	21
Cov. Even. Telegraph	21	8	5	8	48	60	21
Foleshill Social	22	6	4	12	40	71	16
Whitley Wanderers	21	5	5	11	48	58	15
Bridge End	22	6	3	13	46	69	15
WMPTE	22	4	3	15	41	75	11
Walsgrave WMC	20	0	0	20	25	105	0

The Colliers FC
Coventry and District (Sunday) Football League
Senior Division 3 Results 1978/79

Opponents	Res	P	W	D	L	F	A	Pts
Chrysler Sports	L2-3	1	0	0	1	2	3	0
City Treasurers	W8-0	2	1	0	1	10	3	2
Woodlands Ath.	W8-1	3	2	0	1	18	4	4
Renold Chain	W4-1	4	3	0	1	22	5	6
Baginton B.L.	L0-3	5	3	0	2	22	8	6
Post Office Spts.	W3-2	6	4	0	2	25	10	8
Unbrako	W5-1	7	5	0	2	30	11	10
Ryton Bridge	L1-3	8	5	0	3	31	14	10
Barras WMC	L2-4	9	5	0	4	33	18	10
City Treasurers	W5-2	10	6	0	4	38	20	12
Alvis S&S	L1-5	11	6	0	5	39	25	12
Woodlands Ath.	D0-0	12	6	1	5	39	25	13
Barras WMC	W4-2	13	7	1	5	43	27	15
Renold Chain	L2-6	14	7	1	6	45	33	15
Post Office Spts.	W2-1	15	8	1	6	47	34	17
Baginton B.L.	L1-6	16	8	1	7	48	40	17
Chrysler Sports	L1-3	17	8	1	8	49	43	17
Alvis S&S	L1-8	18	8	1	9	50	51	17
Unbrako	D0-0	19	8	2	9	50	51	18
Ryton Bridge		20						
Henley S&S		21						
Henley S&S		22						

The W,D and L results do not agree with the League table at match 19. There is a big discrepancy in the Goals Against columns! Heavy defeat?

Coventry and District (Sunday) Football League
Senior Division 3 Table 1978-79

	P	W	D	L	F	A	Pts
Baginton British Leg'n	19	16	2	1	71	21	34
Renold Chain	20	15	2	3	68	28	32
Chrysler Sports	20	13	1	6	64	45	27
Ryton Bridge	18	14	2	2	80	22	26
Barras WMC	19	10	2	7	57	37	22
Alvis Sports & Social	16	9	1	6	39	25	19
The Colliers	**19**	**8**	**1**	**10**	**52**	**68**	**17**
Post Office Sports	20	8	0	12	51	63	16
Woodlands Athletic	18	4	2	12	29	65	10
Henley S & Social	18	3	2	13	38	59	8
City Treasurers	19	3	1	15	32	93	7
Unbrako	18	2	0	16	21	59	4

Not complete!

Part 6 Events & Inventions
(That rocked the world and would change our lives forever.)

1960
* An earthquake and tsunami (tidal wave) devastated Agadir in Morocco killing 12,000 people.
* OPEC the oil producing nations cartel was formed with a view to increase the price of crude oil.
* Ban the Bomb rally organised by CND (Campaign for NuclearDisamanent) in London attracts 100,000 supporters.
* The USA sends 3,500 troops to Vietnam to support South Vietnam after military escalation from the north.
* Russia shoots down American U2 Spy plane and captures pilot Gary Powers and surveillance photographs of soviet missile sites.
* The Irish Republican Army (IRA) starts its fight against British rule.
* Sir Francis Chichester makes a record solo Atlantic crossing in forty days in his yacht Gypsy Moth 11.
* In the UK the average house price is £2530 and the inflation rate is 1.1%, The MOT is introduced, and Ben Hur, and Psycho is showing at the cinema. Harold Wilson is the Prime Minister, and the Labour Party is the Governing Party.

1961
* Russian Yuri Gagarin is the first human in space, inside his Vostok 1 capsule.
* Cuba declares it is now a communist country and nationalises Land and Businesses including $1 billion US assets.
* Bay of Pigs – the unsuccessful attempt to land 1,500 CIA trained Cuban exiles to overthrow Fidel Castro.
* East German authorities close the border between east and west Berlin and construct the Berlin Wall.
* Britain applies for membership of the EEC (European Economic Community).

* The United Nations General Assembly condemns Aparthied (the Afrikaans word for "separation of white people from others").
* WWF (the World Wide Fund for Nature) started.
* John F Kennedy becomes the 35th President of the United States.

1962
* In the UK, Inflation is 3.6% and a new Ford Cortina would cost you £590.
* The US blockades Cuba after the USSR plans to deploy missiles in Cuba.
President Kennedy and Soviet Premier Khrushchev come to an agreement regarding Cuba, and the missiles are withdrawn as is the blockade.
* American actress, model and singer Marilyn Monroe is found dead, aged 36.
* Brazil beat Czechoslovakia 3-1 to win the World Cup in Chile.
* The Beatles release their first record "Love Me Do"
* Oral Polio Vaccine is developed by Drs Albert Sabin and Jonas Salk.
* Telstar satellite relays the first trans-Atlantic television signal.
* Houston plastic surgeons use silicone breast implants for the first time.

1963
* President John F Kennedy is shot and killed in Dallas by Lee Harvey Oswald, who later kills a policeman. He was arrested soon afterwards and during transportation to the County Jail Oswald is shot and killed by Jack Ruby. Conspiracy theories still discussed today, regarding a second sniper, and Jack Ruby's involvement.
* Martin Luther King delivers his "I have a dream" speech.
* The UK was intrigued by "the Profumo Scandal". John Profumo, the War Minister in the Government, had an affair with a London call girl, Christine Keeler, who was also having an affair with a Russian naval attaché.
* Dr. Beeching recommends closure of 25% of British Rail.

* Pope JohnXX11 dies and the College of Cardinals elect Pope Paul V1.
* The Great Train Robbery takes place; £2.6 million is taken from the Glasgow to London Mail train in a daring raid.
* Conservative Alec Douglas-Home becomes Prime Minister, following Harold MacMillan's resignation.

1964
* US Congress authorises War against North Vietnam, after US Destroyer Maddox was attacked by three North Vietnamese torpedo boats.
* Albert DeSalvo, the Boston Strangler is captured after sexually assaulting and then strangling thirteen women with their nylon stockings.
* Cassius Clay beats Sonny Liston for the World Heavyweight championship.
* The first Ford Mustang rolls off the production lines.
* The British and French governments agree to build a tunnel under the English Channel.
* Mods and Rockers cause disturbances at seaside resorts during the Easter and Whitsun holidays.
* Nelson Mandela and seven others are sentenced to life imprisonment.
* The PLO (Palestine Liberation Organisation) is established with Yasser Arafat as its leader.
* Civil War breaks out in Cyprus, between the Greek and Turkish Cypriots.
* Radio Caroline becomes the first "pirate" radio station.
* The Sun newspaper is published, and Top of the Pops makes its debut on BBC.

1965
* Harold Wilson becomes Prime Minister again after winning the General Election by just five votes.
* BP's Sea Gem rig finds gas in the North Sea

* Rhodesia declares independence from Great Britain and becomes Zimbabwe.
* Australia joins the Vietnam War, and Hindi becomes the official language of
India. Fighting between India and Pakistan escalates.
* Malcom X was shot and killed in Manhattan, he was a member of the Nation of Islam, and taught black supremacy. Years later when his ideals had changed, he left the Nation, and was allegedly killed by his previous supporters.
* The Post Office Tower opened in London.
* 70 mile per hour speed limit imposed on British roads.
* Ranger 9 lands on the moon and sends back live TV broadcasts.
* Russian Cosmonaut, Aleksei Leonov, leaves his spacecraft Voskhod 2, for a 12 minute spacewalk. American Edward H White 11 becomes the second human to walk in space during his flight in Gemini 4.

1966
* Protests against the Vietnam War increase, and Cassius Clay becomes a conscientious objector, and refuses to go to war. He later fought against England's favourite boxer Henry Cooper, who became the first opponent to floor the Louiseville Lip. Henry was to regret that, he was knocked out in five.
* The Aberfan disaster in South Wales; a slag heap high above the little village near Merthyr broke away after five days of heavy rain. The slurry engulfed the Pantglas Junior School and some of the senior school, killing 116 children and 28 adults. It also destroyed twenty houses and farm. Miners from local and nearby collieries worked all day and through the night in the rescue effort.
* The Mini-skirt caused raised eyebrows; Mary Quant reduced the length of her skirts in her shop in the King's Road; she also introduced hot pants.
* The Salvation Army celebrated its centenary.
* England win the World Cup beating Germany 4-2 at Wembley.
* The Moors murderers, Ian Brady and Myra Hindley jailed for life.

* Britain Introduces the first vertical take off and land Aircraft – the Harrier.
* The Hovercraft commences its service across the English Channel.

1967

* The Six Day War; Arab forces attack Israel after Egypt had closed the Strait of Tiran to Israeli shipping. Israel's superior air and land forces destroy any opposition, and secure possession of additional territory.
* Foot and Mouth epidemic spreads across Britain and massive funeral pyres are lit to destroy the animal carcasses.
* The Torrey Canyon, a massive tanker, runs aground off Lands End.
* The Beatles release "Sgt Pepper's Lonely Hearts Club Band"
* Elvis Presley marries Priscilla Wagner.
* The world's first heart transplant, is performed by Dr Christiaan Barnard, in South Africa.
* Gas is pumped ashore at Easington, Co Durham, from the North Sea.
* Barclays Bank installs the first ATM (Automatic Teller Machine)

1968

* Prague Spring - The Soviet Union invades Czechoslovakia and arrest First Secretary Alexander Dubcek and others for the introduction of political reforms contrary to Communist policy.
* Martin Luther King Jr was shot and killed in Memphis by James Earl Ray.
* Dutch Elm disease destroys tens of thousands of trees.
* The Post Office introduce the First Class Post
* London Bridge is sold for £1million and re-erected in Arizona.
* Enoch Powell delivers his "Rivers of Blood" anti-immigration speech.
* The Kray twins were arrested for the murders of Jack 'The Hat' McVitie and George Cornell, members of the London underworld.
* Alec Rose sails around the world single handed in 354 days.
* Aristotle Onassis marries Jacqueline Kennedy.

1969
* Neil Armstrong becomes the first man to set foot on the moon, and utters the famous words "One small step for man, one giant leap for mankind".
* Richard Nixon wins the Presidential Election.
* Live Music Events attract hundreds of thousands in the Summer of Love, at Woodstock (350,000), Atlanta (100,000) and the Isle of Wight (150,000).
* Britain deploys troops in Northern Ireland.
* Invention of the Microprocessor begins the computer revolution.
* "And now for something completely different", yes it's "Monty Pythons Flying Circus" now showing on TV.
* Rolling Stones guitarist Brian Jones is found dead in a swimming pool.

1970
* House prices average £4975 and petrol cost 6s5d a gallon.
* A Cyclone in Bangladesh kills 500,000, and an earthquake in Peru kills 67,000.
* President Nasser of Egypt dies and 5 million mourn his passing.
* The Tanker Pacific Glory spill 100,000 gallons of crude oil in the English Channel, creating an environmental disaster.
* Edward Heath and his Conservative Party win the General Election.
* The Reverend Ian Paisley wins a seat in the Houses of Parliament.

1971
* Inflation has risen to 8.6%
* Both the Britain and Ireland switch to decimal currency.
* Disaster at Ibrox Stadium, after the Rangers and Celtic football match, when 66 people died in a stairway crush.
* Education Secretary Margaret Thatcher ends free milk for children under 7.
* Tsunami in the Bay of Bengal kills 10,000 people
* Idi Amin takes control of Uganda, a notorious dictator!

* Greenpeace is formed, for a peaceful and sustainable world.
* BBC Open University broadcasts begin.
* Oil production commences in the North Sea.

1972
* Arab gunmen (Black September terrorists) kill 11 Israeli athletes at the Munich Olympics and demand release of Palestinians held in Israeli jails.
* The Watergate Scandal – Five White House operatives burglarize and wiretap the offices of the Democratic National Committee.
* The Conservative Government declare a State of Emergency as Miners go on strike and picket Coal fired Power Stations, Steelworks and Ports.
* Explosions in Belfast on "Bloody Friday" kill 9, and injure 130 people. On "Bloody Sunday" British Police gun down 14 unarmed Catholic protestors.
* Idi Amin takes control of British firms and interests in Uganda, and then expels 50,000 Asians from Uganda. Guess where the go to?
* American swimmer, Mark Spitz, wins seven gold medals at the Munich Olympics.
* The Digital Age commences with the sales of Digital Watches, Hand Held Calculators, and Atari consoles with 'Pong' game

1973
* Europe sinks into recession, as OPEC increase the price of oil by 200%, to those countries supporting Israel.
* Britain, Ireland and Denmark join the EEC.
* The World Trade Centre becomes the largest building in the world.
* The IRA commences its mainland bombing campaign, with explosions at Kings Cross and Euston stations, the Old Bailey, and Whitehall.
* The Yom Kippur War was the fourth and largest Arab-Israeli conflict, with Egypt and Syria attempting to recover territory lost in the Six-Day war.

* The British Government impose a three-day working week to save electricity, due to the rising cost of coal and oil through shortages.
* Pink Floyd release The Dark Side of the Moon.
* Princess Anne marries Captain Mark Phillips in Westminster Abbey.

1974
* Richard Nixon resigns as President of the United States following the Watergate Scandal and his involvement. Gerald Ford takes over at the White House.
* The IRA exploded bombs at the Tower of London, and the Houses of Parliament, and also at pubs in Birmingham. An IRA terrorist died in a premature explosion, when planting a bomb at the Telephone Exchange and Postal Sorting Office in Salt Lane, Coventry.
* Israel and Syria agree to a ceasefire, and Turkey invades North Cyprus.
* In Technology, the MRI (Magnetic Resonance Imaging) is developed in the USA, and a primitive Word Processor is introduced into offices, and a Bar Code Scanner is installed in a Supermarket in Ohio.
* The Hung Parliament dissolves and the Labour Party returns to power with Harold Wilson again Prime Minister.

1975
* Uk Inflation rate rises to 24.2% and a gallon of petrol now costs £0.72p.
Margaret Thatcher becomes the first lady leader of the Conservative Party.
* The Vietnam War ends as Communist forces take Saigon, and South Vietnam surrenders unconditionally.
* The IRA murder Ross McWhirter, the co-founder of the Guiness Book of Records.
* The Cod War breaks out between Iceland and Britain, when Iceland extend their fishing rights to 200 miles.
* Bill Gates and Paul Allen develop a BASIC program for the Altair 8800 micro computer, and Microsoft becomes a registered trademark.

* Bic launches the first disposable Razor.
* There is a videotape war as Sony introduces their Betamax system, and JVC/Matsushita their VHS format. Guess who wins?

1976
* An earthquake in Tabgshan in China kills 255,000 people.
* Concorde makes its' first commercial flights from London to Bahrain, and Paris to Rio via Dakar.
* Britain suffers from their worst drought in history.
* James Callaghan becomes Prime Minister when Harold Wilson resigned.
* Black African Nations boycott the Montreal Olympics in protest against the sporting links between South Africa and New Zealand.
* Nadia Comaneci wins 3 gold medals in Gymnastics with 7 perfect scores.
* Palestine extremists hijack an Air France and a Sabena Aircraft, and Israeli commandos storm both planes to free hostage passengers and crew.
* Rioting breaks out at the Notting Hill Carnival.
* At Southend, the world's longest pier (1.34 miles) is destroyed by fire.
* Apple Computer Company is formed by Steve Jobs and Steve Wozniak.
* The first Laser Printer is unveiled by IBM.

1977
* New York City is blacked out due to lightning strikes. It took 25 hours to restore power, during which time there was widespread looting, vandalism and arson, and about 4,000 people had to be evacuated from the subway system.
* Steve Biko, an anti-aparthied activist died in custody in South Africa.
* Jimmy Carter is elected President of the United States of America. He grants a pardon to the draft dodgers in the Vietnam war period.
* The Nobel Peace Prize is awarded to Amnesty International

* A Cyclone in India kills 20,000 and leaves 2 million homeless.
* Britain celebrates the Queens' silver jubilee, 25 years on the throne!
* At the cinema, you had the choice of Star Wars IV; A New Hope, Saturday Night Fever, Rocky or Close Encounters of the Third Kind.

1978
* Public Service strikes cause major disruption to all services.
* European Court of Human Rights finds the UK government guilty of mistreating prisoners in Northern Ireland.
* The US stops production of the Neutron Bomb, which kills people and leave infrastructure standing.
* Pope Paul V1 dies and John Paul 1is elected Pope only to die just 33 days later. Cardinal Karol Wojttyla becomes Pope John Paul 11.
* The Bell Company introduce the first Cellular Mobile Phone System, and Atari Space Invaders launches a craze for Video Games.
* Louise Brown is the first "test tube" baby to be born, using vitro fertilisation.

1979
* USSR invades Afghanistan.
* Margaret Thatcher elected Prime Minister, with a majority of 43 seats.
* The Three Mile Island Nuclear Power Station in Pennsylvania, suffered a partial meltdown due to escape of cooling water.
* Ayatollah Khomeini returns to Iran from exile to seize power. 63 Americans are taken hostage in their Embassy in Tehran. The Iran government becomes an Islamic republic when the Shah of Persia is forced to leave.
* The Sahara desert has a snow fall lasting thirty minutes.
* The Queen's cousin, Lord Mountbatten and three others, are assassinated by an explosion on his boat in Ireland, only hours after 18 soldiers had been killed by booby traps. The IRA are quick to confirm their involvement.

* Conservative MP Airey Neave suffers the same fate in a car-bomb explosion near the Houses of Parliament.
* To control the birth rate in China, the communist party institutes a one child per family rule.
* Sony introduces the Walkman, and VisiCalc is the first spreadsheet program.
* Sid Vicious of the Sex Pistols Punk Rock group dies from a heroin overdose`
* Trivial Pursuit, the general knowledge quiz game hits the shelves.

1980
* The Bank of England Interest is 14%, and Inflation Rate is 18%, and a gallon of petrol is £0.79p
* Iran and Iraq go to war following a long history of border disputes.
* Ronald Reagan elected President of the USA.
* The Iran Embassy in London was seized by terrorists, and 26 hostages held. On the sixth day the terrorists killed a hostage, and the SAS stormed the building, rescuing all but one of the hostages, and killed five of the six terrorists.
* Japan becomes the largest car producing country.
* The Olympic Games in Moscow is boycotted by the US in protest at the Soviet invasion of Afghanistan.
* An earthquake caused the north face of Mount St. Helens in Washington State, to slide away. The eruption that followed killed 57 people, and sent an ash cloud 80,000 feet into the atmosphere.
* Beatle John Lennon is shot dead in New York City, outside the property where he lived, by Mark David Chapman.
* The first domestic Camcorders and Fax machines are on sale in Japan.
* In Mexico, there is the first ever natural birth in captivity of a Giant Panda.
* Millions tune in to watch Dallas, and solve the question "Who shot JR". Yes it was Kristin Shepard, played by Mary Crosby!

A C Godiva 1967/68

Back L to R: - G. Lissaman (Manager), R. Gaulden, J. Colledge, M. Ansell, A. Betts, J. Gair, T. Long, R. Hancox

Front: - R. Munday, J. Donelly, D. Hempshall, G. Smith. R. West

Apollo Rangers 1973/74
Back L to R: - M.Hamill, K.Mullen, J.Colledge, B.Haridence, C.Wyatt, M.Randall, H.Leslie, B.Callaghan, P.Harms. Front L to R: - D.Inkpen, M.Wrighton, B.Caves, R.Shepherd, J.MacHendry, G.Perry, J.Clarke

Barras Green Rangers 1972/73
Back L to R: - B.Clough, D.Hempshall, A.Brick, J.Foley, AN Other,
B.Halcrow, A.Hill, J.Pinnegar (Manager). Front L to R: - P.Johnson,
C.Rust, R.Senior, M.Johns, D.Buckingham, P.Glynn

Barras Green Rangers 1975/76
Back L to R: - B.Thompson, A.Hill. B.Halcrow, J.Foley, P.Glynn, E.Rooney, D.Hempshall, J.Peterson.
Front L to R: - P.Timms, R.Senior, G.Farquharson, T.Foley, K.Mulhearn, K.Foley.

Barras Green WMC 1973/74
Winners of the Tom Cooke Cup, and
Division 2 of the Coventry and Central Warwickshire League.
Alan Hill, Colin Rust, Micky Johns, John Phelan and Dave McOwat, celebrate with Derek Hempshall (Author of Grassroots Football)

Colliers FC 1980/81
Back L to R: -R.Smith, M.McGuigan, L.Anderson, G.Ross, G.Tyrell, P.White, R.Shepherd, C.Hill, A.Goodman. Front L to R: - R.McMillan, S.Williams, P.Hanley, P.McGuire, J.Colledge, V.Wigmore.

Moseley United FC 1964/65 Potters Green 5-a-Side Champions
L to R: - *R.Kimber, J.Colledge, L.Watson, D.Hempshall, A.Setchell.
(*Barry Osbourne of Parkstone WMC played in the competition)

Moseley United FC 1963/64
Back L to R: - G.Bradley, C.Swift, L.Watson, R.Kimber, R.New, J.Colledge, R.Graal, H.Ottley, A.Freeman, P.Webb, J.Crudginton, J.Farquhar, K.Hopkins, J.Sanders. Front L to R: - F.West, D.Hempshall, D.Sephton, I.Hart, P.Hewitt, S.Bradley, A.Setchell, P.Lewis, P.Janes.

Parkstone WMC 'B' 1972/73

Back L to R: - R.Colley, R.Sparkes, B.Bates, M.Wallace, B.Shipton, B.Thomas, M.Hall

Front L to R: - D.Weeks, G.Fletcher, D.Bryson, R.Saye, J.Ashmore.

Derek Hempshall's Collection of Trophies won during 17 years of Grassroots Football.